SELECTED POEMS

CHARLOTTE SMITH was born in 1749 in London, and spent much of her childhood at the family's estate at Bignor Park in Sussex. Her mother died when she was three, and the family's fortunes changed as a result of her father's gambling debts. At the age of fifteen Charlotte Smith married the twenty-three-year-old son of an East India Company merchant. The marriage proved to be a disaster; her husband's profligacy led to seven months' imprisonment in debtors' prison, during which Charlotte Smith accompanied him. The family lived in France for a time following his release, so as to be safe from creditors, but in 1784 Charlotte Smith left her husband. From that point she supported herself and her nine children by her writing. Her *Elegiac Sonnets* were immensely popular and influential, eventually reaching eight editions, but she was also a prolific writer of gothic novels and works for children, a translator and the author of a play. Charlotte Smith died in 1806. Her greatest poem, *Beachy Head*, was published posthumously in 1807.

JUDITH WILLSON is an editor. She studied English at Newnham College, Cambridge and the University of York, and Middle Eastern Studies at the University of Manchester. She has worked as a teacher, and was assistant editor of the *Journal of Semitic Studies* for a number of years.

Fyfield*Books* aim to make available some of the great classics of British and European literature in clear, affordable formats, and to restore often neglected writers to their place in literary tradition.

Fyfield*Books* take their name from the Fyfield elm in Matthew Arnold's 'Scholar Gypsy' and 'Thyrsis'. The tree stood not far from the village where the series was originally devised in 1971.

> *Roam on! The light we sought is shining still.*
> *Dost thou ask proof? Our tree yet crowns the hill,*
> *Our Scholar travels yet the loved hill-side*

from 'Thyrsis'

CHARLOTTE SMITH

Selected Poems

Edited with an introduction by
JUDITH WILLSON

Fyfield*Books*

CARCANET

Acknowledgements

Much of the material about Charlotte Smith's life is drawn from Loraine Fletcher's *Charlotte Smith: A Critical Biography* (Basingstoke and New York, Palgrave 2001). Stuart Curran's *Poems of Charlotte Smith* (New York and Oxford, Oxford University Press 1993) is an essential resource for any reader of Smith's work. I would like to thank Frances Baker of the John Rylands University Library of Manchester, Emma Marigliano of the Portico Library, Manchester, Michael Schmidt, Neil Powell, and Paul, Flora and Edward Willson for their help during the preparation of this book.

First published in Great Britain in 2003 by
Carcanet Press Limited
Alliance House
Cross Street
Manchester M2 7AQ

Introduction and editorial matter © Judith Willson 2003

A CIP catalogue record for this book is available from the British Library
ISBN 1 85754 725 X

The publisher acknowledges financial assistance from Arts Council England

Typeset by XL Publishing Services, Tiverton
Printed and bound in England by SRP Ltd, Exeter

CONTENTS

INTRODUCTION

A woman is kidnapped and imprisoned. Her newborn baby dies. She escapes, attempts suicide, finds shelter in a cave:

> The holly, (1) whose shining thorny and spiny head so much shadowed the whole eminence, had found amidst the roof place for three or four young plants mingling with the larger growth above them; the common bramble (2) crept over another part of it... My walls, which were only partially damp, were tapestried with rock-lichen (7) the tessellated lichen, and the silver bryum (8) ...

> (1) The holly (ilex aquifolium). The beautiful plant with which Burns composed the chaplet of his Scottish muse, (2) Rubus preticasus. There is something particularly elegant in the alternate triple leaves and long weak branches of this plant... (7) Lichen scruposus, (8) Bryum argenteum[1] ...

At this crisis in which a character is poised between life and death, Charlotte Smith gives her readers notes on botany. Smith was a successful novelist: the educational commentary seems an unlikely element in a work characterised by adventures and heightened emotions. But Smith, who knew what made a good story, also knew that the world was not simply scenery against which women's emotional lives were played out. A writer who had experienced a fair number of the traumas an eighteenth-century woman could suffer, and who was tough enough to spend her life keeping one step ahead of them, Smith offers her readers a double narrative. Women who read the novel might identify with the emotional terrain through which the suffering heroine is propelled by plots and cruelties; but they were also being shown that the world has an intricate, objective reality, and that to name and understand its structure is to find a survival strategy.

It is worth approaching Smith through a novel, because to do so shifts the emphasis away from reading her through the diminishing perspective of the later Romantic poets. In the context

vii

of the genre that gave her her status as a professional, working writer, she appears not so much as a lesser precursor, but as a poet arriving at a Romantic understanding of the world from a different direction: from a tradition of women's writing that ranges from childrearing and household management to polemic and pedagogy – and the moral discourse of the novel itself. Charlotte Smith's awkward, accurate cataloguing of the specifics of nature is not only the mark of an imaginative response to nature less fully developed than Wordsworth's: she was interested in knowing, and naming, nature, because to do so was to possess a language for the complex structures by which the world functioned.

This is not a rhetorical point: Smith's own life, and the wider conditions under which women lived, are inextricable from her writing, which was at the simplest level undertaken to pay the rent and to feed her children. Her prefaces to the different editions of her *Elegiac Sonnets* are concerned not with poetic intention, language and imagination, but with increasingly querulous complaints about the odds against her functioning as a writer at all:

> I am compelled to complain of those who have crushed the poor abilities of the *author*, and by the most unheard of acts of injustice *(for twice seven years)* have added the painful sensations of *indignation* to the inconveniences and deprivations of indigence; and aggravating by future dread, the present suffering, have frequently doubled the toil necessary for tomorrow, by palsying the hand and distracting the head, that were struggling against the evils of today![2]

And yet without those pressures she might never have written anything: having an education set her apart from the class of women who worked; having an inescapable financial need to work set her apart from women of her own class, and forced upon her the realities that underpinned conventional moralities. Looking back on the early years of her marriage, she wrote to a friend:

> ...the more my mind expanded, the more I became sensible of personal slavery; the more I improved and cultivated my understanding, the farther I was removed from those with whom I was condemned to pass my life; and the more clearly I

saw by these newly-acquired lights the horror of the abyss into which I had unconsciously plunged.[3]

With even more bitter insight, she wrote that she had been 'sold, a legal prostitute'.[4] Commercial transactions, and the struggle to take control of them, were the continuing themes of a life whose course was determined by her father's and husband's use of the money they controlled or squandered. (Some ten years after she had left her husband – when she was in her forties, experienced in handling her own affairs, a successful writer – it was he who signed the contract for her novel *Desmond* and demanded money from her publishers.) The failure of her marriage reduced her and her children to poverty and social isolation. She worked constantly to keep one step ahead of her creditors, haggled with her publishers, exhausted herself and those around her with the endless legal quarrels with the trust fund that denied her children access to the money they should have inherited. This life had an extraordinarily emblematic quality, bringing her into confrontation with the three great centres of eighteenth-century male power: commerce, property ownership and, overarching both, the law. A passage from *The Hardships of the English Laws in Relation to Wives*, published in 1735 to educate women about their legal position, might have been written for the young Charlotte Smith, and for the more naïve readers of her novels:

> If we reflect how extreamly ignorant all young Women are as to points in Law, and how their Education and Way of Life, shuts them out from the Knowledge of their true Interest in almost all things, we shall find that their Trust and Confidence in the Man they love, and Inability to make use of the proper Means to guard against his Falsehood, leave few in a Condition to make use of that Precaution.[5]

Only her intelligence, her ability to deal with the institutions ranged against her, enabled her and the family to survive, barely. The hard reality that set her apart from the later Romantic poets was the understanding that for women to elevate the private world of feeling could be a dangerous trap, leaving them ill-equipped for survival. Her passionate exactitude both recognises and celebrates the complexity of the external world.

Charlotte Smith was born on 4 May 1749 in her father's London town house, the second daughter of Nicholas and Anna Turner. Her father owned two estates, Stoke Place near Guildford in Surrey and Bignor Park in Sussex; both these landscapes feature in her later writing. Her mother died when Charlotte was three years old. The children were then brought up by their unmarried aunt while their father travelled abroad for some years, dividing their time between Bignor Park, the London house and school. Charlotte was educated first at a school in Chichester, where she was taught the polite accomplishments of painting and drawing by George Smith, a landscape painter of some note. At eight she moved on to a girls' school in Kensington, which seems to have prepared her to be precisely the eligible match that she shortly became. There is more than a touch of Becky Sharp in the clever, self-confident schoolgirl recalled, not altogether fondly, by a contemporary:

> ...she excelled most of us in writing and drawing. She was reckoned by far the finest dancer, and was always brought forward for exhibition when company was assembled to see our performances; and she would have excelled all her competitors, but she was always thought *too great a genius* to study. She had a great taste for music, and a correct ear, but never applied it with sufficient steadiness to ensure success... She had read more than anyone in school, and was continually composing verses...[6]

Around this time the family suffered the kind of reversal of fortunes that haunted the security of eighteenth-century women, in fiction and in reality, knowing as they did that their lives were defined by family status and their security depended upon the good sense or good luck of fathers and husbands. The town house, the country estates, the girls' fashionable education, were revealed to have no solid foundations. Nicholas Turner sold Stoke Place, and sold or mortgaged other properties, to meet his gambling debts. Charlotte was taken out of school at the age of twelve and 'was at that very early age introduced into society, frequented all public places with her family, and her appearance and manners were so much beyond her years, that at fourteen her father received proposals for her from a gentleman of suitable station and fortune'.[7] The girls, like the land, were assets whose value it was now time to realise. In fact, it would be a few more years before

Charlotte was married. In October 1764 Nicholas Turner married a rich heiress; in February 1765 his fifteen-year-old daughter married Benjamin Smith, the twenty-three-year-old son of a wealthy director of the East India Company. Later recollections ascribed the marriage to the jealousy of the wicked stepmother and the foolish contrivances of the spinster aunt who had taken on the thankless task of raising her brother-in-law's family: this sounds like an imposed narrative. The reality was that her father's remarriage displaced his daughter from her place in the family, and her expectation of inheritance, as it did his unmarried sister-in-law. Their best hope of security lay in marriage. Lucy Towers, the aunt, who seems to have exchanged the life of a dependant in Nicholas Turner's household for a comparable role in Charlotte's, finally achieved status and security in 1767 when she married Richard Smith, Charlotte Smith's widowed father-in-law. For Charlotte the gamble failed: Benjamin Smith was a spendthrift, dissolute idler, dissipating the profits of his merchant father's trade.

The newly married couple lived at first close to the Turners' warehouse in London, and subsequently in a village within travelling distance of the city. Here three children were born; of the two who had been born in London, one had already died in infancy. Charlotte gave birth to eight children in the first nine years of marriage; of twelve pregnancies, nine children in all survived to adulthood. A memoir by her sister, Catherine Dorset, records Smith's growing understanding of her own unhappiness in the early years of her marriage:

> She began to trace that indefatigable restlessness and impatience, of which she had long been conscious without comprehending, to its source, to discriminate characters, to detect ignorance, to compare her own mind with those of the persons by whom she was surrounded.
>
> The consciousness of her own superiority, the mortifying conviction that she was subjected to one so infinitely her inferior, presented itself every day more forcibly to her mind...[8]

Interestingly, Charlotte Smith and her father-in-law seem to have struck up an affectionate relationship; she appears to have taken an interest in the business, as her husband signally failed to do. According to Catherine Dorset, Richard Smith even offered her an allowance if she would remain in London and assist him. The social categories were slippery – Charlotte Turner may have spent her childhood in a brief period of her family's landed prosperity, but her background was distinctly insecure; the Smiths were on the precarious way up from trade. When Charlotte and Benjamin Smith moved in 1774 to Lys Farm, a country estate in Hampshire, it was Richard Smith's mercantile profits that underpinned the investment in land. (The earliest of the poems that would eventually be published as Smith's *Elegiac Sonnets* date from this period at Lys Farm in the late 1770s.) The purchase was part of Richard Smith's attempt at the end of his life both to protect the assets of his business and to find some occupation for his son. As if to give physical expression to a metaphor of social climbing and moral decline, the Smiths began to spend Richard Smith's profits on transforming the estate from a working farm into a landscaped park.

Richard Smith died in 1776, leaving each of his grandchildren with an annuity and a lump sum, due to them when they came of age or married, to be administered in the meantime by trustees. Benjamin, overseen by the trustees, was responsible for settling the firm's accounts and for ensuring that the annuities were paid. In attempting to safeguard his assets from being spent or sold off by his son, though, Richard Smith had created a will of such impenetrable complexity that attempts to claim her children's inheritance from the trustees would dominate the rest of Charlotte Smith's life. With no property of her own held in trust for her before marriage (which would have ensured that it could have passed directly to her children), a husband who wasted the assets his father had accumulated, and no means to pursue litigation, she was trapped by her father's and her husband's failures. Powerlessness, and desperation, made her relentless in pursuit of anyone who might take up her cause with the trustees. The prefaces to succeeding editions of her *Elegiac Sonnets* provide a vivid record of her anger, publication giving force to the traditional woman's weapon of bitter words:

The time is indeed arrived, when I have been promised by 'the Honourable Men' who *nine years ago*, undertook to see that my family obtained the provision their grandfather designed for them… Still to receive – not a repetition of promises indeed – but of *scorn and insult* when I apply to those gentlemen, who, though they acknowledge that all impediments to a division of the estate they have undertaken to manage are done away – will neither tell me *when* they will proceed to divide it, or *whether they will ever do so at all.*[9]

Litigation in the end became self-devouring, as the estate was depleted by legal fees; it would be thirty-seven years before the surviving beneficiaries were able to claim what remained of their inheritance. In the short term, the Smiths' way of life was sustained for some years by the government contracts that Benjamin Smith secured during the American War of Independence, but the income ended with the war in 1782. Less than a year later, he was arrested for debt and embezzlement from the trust fund. Charlotte Smith left her children with her younger brother and spent much of the next seven months with him in the King's Bench Prison. With the energy and competence that would mark the rest of her life, she dealt with lawyers and negotiated with creditors; she secured a release for her husband and, when the creditors returned, she used the French she had learned at her fashionable school to find him lodgings in France out of their immediate reach, travelling to Dieppe and back in a day. And more than this; in 1784 she took the step of having the *Elegiac Sonnets* printed:

> Some very melancholy moments have been beguiled by expressing in verse the sensations those moments brought. Some of my friends with partial indiscretion, have multiplied the copies they procured… till they found their way into the prints of the day in a mutilated state; which, concurring with other circumstances, determined me to put them into their present form.[10]

As Loraine Fletcher points out in her critical biography, the plea is conventional, and sustains Smith's position as a modestly reticent amateur and, more particularly, as a modest woman reluctantly forced into the limelight. In fact, she went to some lengths to find a publisher for the sonnets and to secure the endorsement of William Hayley, a neighbour and popular poet who would remain her patron. It is notable too that she identified herself as the author 'Charlotte Smith of Bignor Park', her childhood home and, for a woman whose most recent address had been a prison, a mark of both gentility and independent identity.

Like the content of the sonnets themselves, which transmute the landscape of the country estate, the death of children and financial insecurity into the familiar, delicate melancholies of Arcadia, the pose gives an acceptable form to the reality that she needed money.

The sonnets did well, and a second edition followed within a year. In all, there would be ten further editions, to which poems were added over the years. One literary echo may suggest something of what made the sonnets so popular. In *Persuasion*, Anne Elliot, at a low moment

> could not immediately fall into a quotation again. The sweet scenes of autumn were for a while put by – unless some tender sonnet, fraught with the apt analogy of the declining year, with declining happiness, and the images of youth and hope, and spring, all gone together, blessed her memory.[11]

In her introduction to Smith's novel *Emmeline*, Anne Ehrenpreis suggests that this is an allusion to one of the *Elegiac Sonnets*, perhaps specifically to sonnet II, one of Smith's distinctively miserable responses to spring:

> The garlands fade that spring so lately wove
>   Each simple flower which she had nursed in dew…
> Another May new buds and flowers shall bring;
> Ah! Why has happiness no second spring?

If this is so, then there is a sense here of a dialogue between women writers, of Jane Austen's understanding that Smith's sonnets of loss and solitude were particularly expressive of a female character whose lost opportunity for marriage has dislocated her in the social network. And while the figure of the sensitive solitary was conventional, the sonnets' landscape of lonely wilderness has a particular resonance, both fearful and enticing, for women defined by their place in a smaller, social world:

> O'er the dark waves the winds tempestuous howl;
>   The screaming sea-bird quits the troubled sea:
>   But the wild gloomy scene has charms for me,
> And suits the mournful temper of my soul.[12]

As much as her gothic novels gave women readers metaphors for their institutional powerlessness and dangerous emotional autonomy, the sonnets dignified women's private experiences of nostalgia for childhood freedoms and home, their grief at the death of children, by giving their loss a formal poetic shape:

> Sighing I see yon little troop at play,
>   By sorrow yet untouched, unhurt by care;
> While free and sportive they enjoy today,
>   'Content and careless of tomorrow's fare!'
> O happy age! When hope's unclouded ray
>   Lights their green path...[13]

In its decorous, conventional formal skill there is an obvious sense in which a woman is here consciously appropriating the poetic role. But the sudden simplicity of that 'green path' does something more, creating a glowing centre to the sonnet, animating with a vivid particularity what might have been merely imitative skill .

In the formality of the sonnets, Smith can be seen finding a language for female experience within poetic conventions. In sonnet XCI, 'Reflections on Some Drawings of Plants', she takes the traditional equation of the fragility of blossoms and young life, and the enduring power of art to celebrate them, and realises them as specifically female metaphors of experience: the feminine accomplishment of flower painting, the daughter who dies leaving no public trace of her existence:

> I can in groups these mimic flowers compose,
>   These bells and golden eyes, embathed in dew;
> Catch the soft blush that warms the early rose,
>   Or the pale iris cloud with veins of blue;
> Copy the scalloped leaves, and downy stems,
>   And bid the pencil's varied shades arrest
> Spring's humid buds, and summer's musky gems:
>   But, save the portrait on my bleeding breast,
> I have no semblance of that form adored, ...
>   That grief, my angel! With too faithful art
>   Enshrines thy image in thy mother's heart.

The art of the flower-painter is meticulous and decorative, a skill that makes no claim to the seriousness of the high tradition of (male) art. In Smith's sonnet, the miniaturising prettiness becomes an expression of women's silenced experiences, the unarticulated grief that breaks out into that 'bleeding breast' which is both poetically conventional and shockingly unfeminine. The narrow focus has itself become a means of looking, and interpreting.

To consider another female perspective. In *Northanger Abbey*, Henry Tilney instructs Catherine Morland in how to look at landscape. He 'talked of fore-grounds, distances, and second distances – side-screens and perspectives – lights and shades'.[14] He is teaching her how to interpret a landscape in the most conventional, approved manner, as a series of pleasingly arranged surfaces, seen as wide views: implied is a proprietorial attitude both to landscape and to Catherine's artless enjoyment of the countryside. The educated eye selects and shapes the natural world according to defined formulae; from the right vantage point, all discordant detail can be smoothed out, leaving a harmonious, distant prospect. (Too eager to learn the approved response to nature, Catherine famously dismisses the entire city of Bath as unworthy of its place in the landscape.) The formal classicism of the eighteenth-century landscape painter merges here with the Romantic identification between the mountain top and the aspiration towards the infinite – both enable the poet to the rise above the details that are a barrier to sublimity. In what is perhaps the closest she came to an explication of her literary beliefs, in her educational works for children (*Rural Walks*, *Rambles Further* and *Conversations Introducing Poetry*), Smith explicitly rejects the wide viewpoint for an understanding of the minute particulars of nature. Her (female) narrator teaches the child that to understand nature she must look at the detailed structure of the landscape for herself, not learn the correct responses to 'prospects'. Smith's notes to the poems that appear in these works are sometimes longer than the poems themselves; together they seamlessly encompass both accurate observation and a sense of wonder at the extraordinariness of nature:

> Small, viewless æronaut, that by the line*
> Of gossamer suspended, in mid air
> Float'st on a sunbeam – living atom, where
> Ends thy breeze-guided voyage

> * The almost imperceptible threads floating in the air, towards

the end of Summer or Autumn, in still evening, sometimes are so numerous as to be felt on the face and hands. It is on these that a minute species of spider convey themselves from place to place; sometimes rising with the wind to a great height in the air…

In the first edition of *Conversations Introducing Poetry*, a further note, omitted when 'To the Insect of the Gossamer' was included in the *Elegiac Sonnets*, recounts Gilbert White's observation of the same phenomenon in the *Natural History of Selbourne*.[15] Smith's writing shares with White's the freshness of an enquiring intelligence finding new ways of looking: the same delight in accuracy, informed by a sensibility that finds meaning in the truth of observed detail. She is moved by the objective reality of nature, and through it finds a language to articulate the relationship between human life and the processes of nature. At its best, Smith's precision achieves a transformative understanding that is closer to scientific thought than to the imitation of poetic forms. It looks forward to Romanticism, and to the kind of empathy with the diverse particularity of the world to which Romanticism gave a voice, but for Smith as a woman writer there is a particular meaning in rejecting a generalising, distanced imagery of nature. For a woman, to look closely was to challenge received truths: ignorance preserves innocence. Just how radical Smith was is made clear in a comparison not just with such amusing oddities as Richard Polwhele's 'The Unsex'd Females' (who 'With bliss botanic as their bosoms heave/Still pluck forbidden fruit with mother Eve') but with another woman writer, Smith's near-contemporary, Anna Barbauld. Like Smith, Barbauld inherits a long tradition of associations between natural and female innocence and beauty:

Flowers, the sole luxury which nature knew,
In Eden's pure and guiltless garden grew.
To loftier forms are tougher tasks assign'd…
But this soft family, to cares unknown,
Were born for pleasure and delight alone.
Gay without toil, and lovely without art,
They spring to cheer the sense, and glad the heart.[16]

Setting Barbauld's 'To a Lady, with some painted flowers' beside

Smith's 'Reflections on Some Drawings of Plants' is to see not only how delicately unforced is Smith's identification between the woman's flower-painting and her lost child, but simply how much better informed she is about nature. Her flowers are particularly and objectively themselves before they are symbols of anything. One feels cheered by the thought of a child given a copy of *Rural Walks* or *Conversations Introducing Poetry* in the 1790s, being taught not piety and modest conduct but to go and look enquiringly at the world.

The *Elegiac Sonnets* made Smith little money – she had paid for the printing of the first edition herself, and so had to repay the publisher from the profits – but, from the standpoint of a modern reader, they mark the point from which she can be defined as a writer. To an extent, this is a distortion: her verse, while more than private, was never central to her financial independence. Yet it is clear that at this time she saw her intellectual ability as a practical and calculated means of survival.

In 1784, pregnant for the twelfth time, she took the entire family to join her husband in Normandy, where they spent six months in what seems to have been an all too authentically gothic castle, complete with snowstorms and sinister monks. It was here that she began to write for money, translating Prévost's novel *Manon L'Éscaut*. The family returned to England in the spring, and Smith began a translation of a selection from a book of legal cases, *Les causes célèbres*, which she entitled *The Romance of Real Life* (and which included the first English version of *The Return of Martin Guerre*). Both books had the elements for good sales, as she must have known: strong stories and controversial content. *Manon* was soon withdrawn from publication following an accusation of plagiarism, but the legal cases sold well enough to support the family for eighteen months. By now, Benjamin Smith had returned to France alone, although he came back to England to plague her sporadically. Charlotte Smith was now solely responsible for supporting herself and the children, who had chosen to remain with her (legally, had her husband claimed them, she would have had no rights to them).

From this point she would be, as Cowper saw her, 'chained to her desk like a slave to his oar',[17] although she seems to have been more robust than the image suggests. She became a confident professional writer, demanding advances from her publishers and berating them for shoddy typesetting. From 1788 she published a three- or four-volume novel almost every year for ten years, while contriving to pay off creditors, keeping the children alive through dangerous illnesses or mourning their deaths. She established the boys in army careers and the girls in marriages, always trapped in the relentless pursuit of the annuities that would give them financial security. She was constantly on the verge of real poverty; she had to care for a son who had been terribly wounded at the Siege of Dunkirk, and a daughter who returned home from a violent marriage with her two small children; she lost another daughter, believing that she might have lived had she had the money to pay for her medical care; towards the end of her life she sold her library to pay the bills. With good reason, Southey wrote that she 'is more humanised, more akin to common feelings, than most literary women'.[18] Her lived experience of catastrophe, displacement and insecurity, which might have destroyed her, instead drove her to look, to make connections between her individual struggle and the wider world, to find the significance in details, to understand the ways in which the outsider was both unprotected and free.

If the *Elegiac Sonnets* maintain at least a pretence of being private outpourings forced into public, *The Emigrants* marks a confident engagement with the changing currents of ideas around her. In 1792 Smith had published *Desmond*, a novel of romantic passion and oppressive marriage set during the French Revolution. The setting was more than background colour; Smith had visited Paris in 1791 while working on the novel, and defended her interpretation of the political issues in her preface to the novel:

> Even in the commonest course of female education, they are expected to acquire some knowledge of history; and yet if they are to have no opinion of what *is* passing it avails little that they should be informed of what *has passed*, in a world where they are subject to such mental degradation; where they are censured as affecting masculine knowledge if they happen to have any understanding.[19]

In *The Emigrants* (1793) Smith's understanding of the political cataclysm in France is to see that it may be played out in individual lives not as a triumph for freedom but as a struggle for survival when all the certainties have gone. The poem's evident sympathy for the feudal chief and 'one whose only crime / Was being born a monarch' is less anti-revolutionary than post-revolutionary, written at the moment when the slogans lose their purity.

The poem is very precisely located, Book I in November 1792, immediately following the September massacres of moderates and counter-revolutionaries, and Book II in April 1793, following the execution of King Louis XVI and the imprisonment of his family in January, and the declaration of war between England and France in February. The emigrants are those women, children and clergy who had fled France in 1792 – the incidental victims of history. There is an extraordinary engagement with developing events: at this time Smith herself was giving shelter to French refugees who had crossed the Channel. Marie Antoinette would be executed only a few weeks after the work's publication. Set against the local detail is Smith's wider vision of loss and displacement as both historical and timeless. From the opening lines of the poem, on the cliffs looking out over the English Channel onto an elementally bleak world of waves, wind and stone, Smith writes with sweeping authority. Here, on a grander scale than in the sonnets, her receptiveness to the melancholy beauty of grey and wintry landscapes becomes an expression of the desolation of lives silenced by exile, and her borrowings from Shakespeare, Milton and Virgil lend weighty voices to the poem's vision of the historical moment. The epigraph for Book II, Virgil's vision of a world laid waste by war, where right and wrong are no longer distinguishable, suggests a universality of suffering, and the figures who appear in the poem have an ahistorical, monumental quality. But what makes the poem so compelling is Smith's command of scale and focus, from the grand and universal to the personal and circumstantial: war seen in the perspective of the 'mimic navy' of the children playing on the beach while their mother anxiously watches for a ship from France. At the centre of the poem is a continuity not only between contemporary history and universal themes, but between Smith's individual experience, the 'complicated woes' to which she returns at the end of the poem, and the fate of those uprooted by great political events. The poem's landscape has all Smith's accuracy of observed detail; it is also the landscape of unconsoled exile, haunted by memories of other times and places. In evoking long vistas of time in which the suffering of the powerless is a constant, Smith transforms epic into a bleak memorial to unrecorded lives overwhelmed by history:

Poor wand'ring wretches! Whoso'er ye are,
That hopeless, houseless, friendless, travel wide
O'er these bleak russet downs; where, dimly seen,
The solitary shepherd shiv'ring tends
His dun discoloured flock…[20]

The wandering wretches and the solitary shepherd, setting off on their long trudge through Romantic poetry, are the product of an understanding of history from a very specific perspective of powerlessness.

In her last years, Charlotte Smith seems to have been exhausted by worry and overwork; she was crippled by rheumatism, in pain and hardly able to walk or write. Her last novel was published in 1802; she then wrote three children's books, including the *Conversations Introducing Poetry*, partly in collaboration with Catherine Dorset, who was establishing herself as a children's writer. Dorset's memoir depicts Charlotte Smith occasionally writing in the family sitting room, surrounded by grandchildren, cheerful although incapacitated. What is missing from this soothing account of a sad decline is the fact that her most powerful and ambitious poem, *Beachy Head*, published posthumously in 1807, also dates from this time. Written from the confines of that family room, it is before anything else a soaring, exhilarating celebration of the unconfined imagination. Smith creates dizzying vistas of space and geological time from the summit of the cliff she could no longer have climbed: night fading as the sun rises over the sea, the 'vast concussion' as continents form. The apparent theme is conventional: all history leads to the triumph of the free and independent English, sturdy repellers of invasion from the time of the Romans, ready to stand against the threat from the Continent again in 1806. It is public history, brightly coloured and noisy – 'The enervate sons of Italy may yield… / Never, never thou! / Imperial mistress of the obedient sea'. What Smith makes of this child's history of England narrative, though, is something far more compelling.

Occasionally awkward with precise terminology ('the Saxon heptarchy'), loaded with notes on the history of France in the ninth century or the habitat of the yellow wagtail, *Beachy Head* often reads as if Smith is writing an encyclopaedia of her imagination. Few poems with such an epic subject convey so immediate a sense of unfolding within the mind of the author. An account of traces of Roman camps found on the Downs leads her to imagine 'the huge unwieldy elephant' brought from Africa with the legions to die of cold in England. From there, she digresses into a note recounting the discovery of elephant bones in Sussex in 1740 – some were kept at Burton House, others in the possession of the Rev. Dr Langrish, who dated them to the time of the Flood. She writes that she never saw them herself, and now has no books to refer to, then remembers that in the National Museum in Paris she saw huge elephant bones, which had been discovered in North America, before adding that since writing the note she has been told that rhinoceros bones have also been found in America. Meanwhile, the poem itself has moved on, and the notes loop back to meet it with an account of peasants' belief that the bones are those of giants, and the place names associated with such beliefs. Her non-linear, associative, diachronic mode constantly diverts the poem, focusing on lovingly realised detail – the creeping thyme in the close-cropped downland grass, the sound of the mill-race at dusk – inventing poems within the poem, capturing memories, making connections between past and present, private and public. It is perhaps a peculiarly female language, blurring the grand narrative into multiplicity. It might have collapsed into wordy incoherence. What is striking, though, is not that *Beachy Head* is garrulous, or shapeless, but that it is modern. This is a poem that proceeds with the rhythms and directions of thought, that is constantly on the point of breaking out of linearity, each meticulously recorded detail part of a web of experiences. Its great vistas encompass personal memories and national history; the Downs covered by sea in the vastness of geological time and the farmer's boy setting bird traps in the August 'floods of corn'.

The poem is almost certainly unfinished, and the ending may be more haunting than Smith ever intended. Thirty years before, she explains in a note, she heard the story of a man called Darby who lived in a cave under the cliff, and drowned one night in a storm while attempting to rescue shipwrecked sailors. In *Beachy Head*, the hermit performs the final duty of praying for the drowned; in his turn shepherds search his cave after the storm and bury him. The final loneliness of the individual death, the vastness of nature, and the need to memorialise create an unspoken community of the displaced and independent. From its opening on the cliff's 'stupendous summit', the poem finds its perhaps unintended ending in the silent tableau in the cave.

Charlotte Smith died in 1806 at Tilford, Surrey, close to Stoke Place, one of the family estates of her childhood. She is buried in the church of Stoke-next-Guildford, near her mother's tomb, as she had requested. Her family erected a plaque to her, and tradition considers a dull poem, conveniently titled 'To My Lyre', to be her last work. A better memorial than either is her recollection of herself in *Beachy Head*, climbing the sheep paths of the Downs as a young girl, noting with luminous precision the tufts of sheep wool caught on the thorn hedges, the carter jamming a stone under a wheel to rest his team, and how after rain the clear streams turn grey and chalky.

Notes

1. Charlotte Smith, *The Young Philosopher*, vol. II (London, Cadell and Davies 1798), pp. 32–3, quoted in Loraine Fletcher, *Charlotte Smith: A Critical Biography* (Basingstoke and New York, Palgrave 2001), pp. 268–9.
2. Charlotte Smith, preface to *Elegiac Sonnets*, vol. II (London, Thomas Cadell 1797), in Stuart Curran (ed.), *The Poems of Charlotte Smith* (New York and Oxford, Oxford University Press 1993), p. 9.
3. Charlotte Smith, undated letter, quoted in Fletcher, *Charlotte Smith*, p. 38.
4. Charlotte Smith, letter, 15 June 1804, quoted in Fletcher, *Charlotte Smith*, p. 25.
5. Sarah Chapone, *The Hardships of the English Laws in Relation to Wives* (London, W. Bowyer 1735), p. 33, quoted in Gillian Skinner, 'Women's Status as Legal and Civic Subjects: "A Worse Condition than Slavery Itself"', in Vivien Jones (ed.), *Women and Literature in Britain 1700–1800* (Cambridge, Cambridge University Press 2000), pp. 91–110, pp. 99–100.
6. From Catherine Anne Dorset's memoir of her sister, quoted in Fletcher, *Charlotte Smith*, p. 14.
7. Ibid., p. 19.
8. Ibid., p. 37.
9. Charlotte Smith, Preface to sixth edition of *Elegiac Sonnets* (London, Thomas Cadell 1792), in Curran, *Poems*, pp. 5–6.
10. Charlotte Smith, Preface to the first and second editions of *Elegiac Sonnets* (London, J. Dodsley 1784), in Curran, *Poems*, p. 3.
11. Jane Austen, *Persuasion*, ed. D.W. Harding (Harmondsworth, Penguin Books 1980), p. 107.

12. Charlotte Smith, sonnet XXI.

13. Charlotte Smith, sonnet XXVII.

14. Jane Austen, *Northanger Abbey*, ed. Anne Henry Ehrenpreis (Harmondsworth, Penguin Books 1978), p. 125.

15. Curran, *Poems*, p. 66.

16. Anna Barbauld, 'To a Lady, with some painted flowers', quoted in Harriet Guest, 'Eighteenth-Century Femininity: A Supposed Sexual Character', in Jones, *Women and Literature in Britain 1700–1800*, pp. 46–68, p. 48. Polewhele is quoted in Fletcher, *Charlotte Smith*, p. 233.

17. Fletcher, *Charlotte Smith*, p. 163.

18. Robert Southey, letter to Charles Danvers, quoted in Fletcher, *Charlotte Smith*, p. 289.

19. Charlotte Smith, Preface to *Desmond* (London, G.G.J. and J. Robinson 1792).

20. *The Emigrants*, I, 296–300.

NOTE ON THE TEXTS

The text of poems taken from *Elegiac Sonnets and Other Poems* is based on the two-volume edition of 1797, which comprised the eighth edition of volume I and the first of volume II (London, T. Cadell and W. Davies). The text of *The Emigrants* is based on the first edition (London, T. Cadell 1793), as is that of the poems taken from *Conversations Introducing Poetry* (London, J. Johnson 1804) and *Beachy Head and Other Poems* (London, J. Johnson 1807).

Capitalisation, and occasionally punctuation, have been modernised, as has spelling. Most of Smith's copious notes have been omitted; where included they appear in the endnotes to the text.

FURTHER READING

Anderson, John, 'Beachy Head: The Romantic Fragment Poem', Huntington Library Quarterly 63, no. 4, available online at www.huntington.org/HLPress/HEHPubs.html

Curran, Stuart, 'Romantic Poetry: The I Altered', in Anne K. Mellor (ed.), Romanticism and Feminism, Bloomington and Indianapolis, Indiana University Press 1988, pp. 185–207

Curran, Stuart, 'Women Readers, Women Writers', in Stuart Curran (ed.), The Cambridge Companion to British Romanticism, Cambridge, Cambridge University Press 1993, pp. 177–95

Curran, Stuart (ed.), The Poems of Charlotte Smith, New York and Oxford, Oxford University Press 1993

Doody, Margaret Anne, 'Women Poets of the Eighteenth Century', in Vivien Jones (ed.), Women and Literature in Britain 1700–1800, Cambridge, Cambridge University Press 2000, pp. 217–37

Fay, Elizabeth A., A Feminist Introduction to Romanticism, Malden, MA and Oxford, Blackwell 1998

Ferguson, Moira, Eighteenth-Century Women Poets: Nation, Class and Gender, New York, State University of New York Press 1995

Fletcher, Loraine, Charlotte Smith: A Critical Biography, Basingstoke and New York, Palgrave 2001

Jones, Vivien (ed.), Women and Literature in Britain 1700–1800, Cambridge, Cambridge University Press 2000

Kelly, Gary, Women, Writing, and Revolution 1790–1827, Oxford, Clarendon Press 1993

Mellor, Anne K., Romanticism and Gender, New York and London, Routledge 1993

Pascoe, Judith, 'Female Botanists and the Poetry of Charlotte Smith' in Carlo Shiner Wilson and Joel Haefner (eds), Revisioning Romanticism, Philadelphia, University of Pennsylvania Press 1994, pp. 193–209

Wolfson, Susan J., 'Charlotte Smith's Emigrants: Forging Connections at the Borders of a Female Tradition', Huntington Library Quarterly 63, no. 4, available online at www.huntington.org/HLPress/HEHPubs.html

From *Elegiac Sonnets and Other Poems*

I

The partial Muse has from my earliest hours
    Smiled on the rugged path I'm doomed to tread,
And still with sportive hand has snatched wild flowers,
    To weave fantastic garlands for my head:
But far, far happier is the lot of those   5
    Who never learned her dear delusive art;
Which, while it decks the head with many a rose,
    Reserves the thorn, to fester in the heart.
For still she bids soft Pity's melting eye
    Stream o'er the hills she knows not to remove,   10
 Points every pang, and deepens every sigh
    Of mourning friendship, or unhappy love.
Ah! then, how dear the Muse's favours cost,
If those paint sorrow best – who feel it most!

II
Written at the Close of Spring

The garlands fade that spring so lately wove,
    Each simple flower, which she had nursed in dew,
Anemones, that spangled every grove,
    The primrose wan, the harebell mildly blue.
No more shall violets linger in the dell,   5
    Or purple orchis variegate the plain,
Till spring again shall call forth every bell,
    And dress with humid hands her wreaths again.
Ah! poor humanity! So frail, so fair,
    Are the fond visions of thy early day,   10
Till tyrant passion, and corrosive care,
    Bid all thy fairy colours fade away!
Another May new buds and flowers shall bring;
Ah! why has happiness – no second spring?

IV
To the Moon

Queen of the silver bowl – by thy pale beam,
    Alone and pensive, I delight to stray,
And watch thy shadow trembling in the stream,
    Or mark the floating clouds that cross thy way.
And while I gaze, thy mild and placid light   5
    Sheds a soft calm upon my troubled breast;
And oft I think – fair planet of the night,
    That in thy orb, the wretched may have rest:
The sufferers of the earth perhaps may go,
    Released by death – to thy benignant sphere,   10
And the sad children of despair and woe
    Forget in thee, their cup of sorrow here.
Oh! that I soon may reach thy world serene,
Poor wearied pilgrim – in this toiling scene!

V
To the South Downs

Ah! hills beloved! – where once, a happy child,
    Your beechen shades, 'your turf, your flowers among',
I wove your bluebells into garlands wild,
    And woke your echoes with my artless song.
Ah! hills beloved! – your turf, your flowers remain;   5
    But can they peace to this sad breast restore,
For one poor moment sooth the sense of pain,
    And teach a breaking heart to throb no more?
And you, Aruna! – in the vale below,
    As to the sea your limpid waves you bear,   10
Can you one kind Lethean cup bestow,
    To drink a long oblivion to my care?
Ah! no! – when all, e'en hope's last ray is gone,
There's no oblivion – but in death alone!

VII
On the Departure of the Nightingale

Sweet poet of the woods – a long adieu!
    Farewell, soft minstrel of the early year!
Ah! 'twill be long ere thou shalt sing anew,
    And pour thy music on 'the night's dull ear'.
Whether on spring thy wandering flights await,   5
    Or whether silent in our groves you dwell,
The pensive muse shall own thee for her mate,
    And still protect the song she loves so well.
With cautious step, the lovelorn youth shall glide
    Thro' the lone brake that shades thy mossy nest;   10
And shepherd girls from eyes profane shall hide
    The gentle bird, who sings of pity best:
For still thy voice shall soft affections move,
And still be dear to sorrow, and to love!

XII
Written on the Sea Shore – October, 1784

On some rude fragment of the rocky shore,
    Where on the fractured cliff the billows break,
    Musing, my solitary seat I take,
And listen to the deep and solemn roar.

O'er the dark waves the winds tempestuous howl;   5
    The screaming seabird quits the troubled sea:
    But the wild gloomy scene has charms for me,
And suits the mournful temper of my soul.

Already shipwrecked by the storms of fate,
    Like the poor mariner methinks I stand,   10
    Cast on a rock; who sees the distant land
From whence no succour comes – or comes too late.
Faint and more faint are heard his feeble cries,
'Till in the rising tide the exhausted sufferer dies.

XXII
To Solitude
(Supposed to be written by Werther)

Oh, Solitude! to thy sequestered vale
    I come to hide my sorrow and my tears,
And to thy echoes tell the mournful tale
    Which scarce I trust to pitying Friendship's ears!
Amidst thy wild woods, and untrodden glades,   5
    No sounds but those of melancholy move;
And the low winds that die among thy shades,
    Seem like soft Pity's sighs for hopeless love!
And sure some story of despair and pain,
    In yon deep copse, thy murm'ring doves relate;   10
And, hark! methinks in that long plaintive strain,
    Thine own sweet songstress weeps my wayward fate!
Ah, nymph! That fate assist me to endure,
And bear awhile – what death alone can cure!

XXVI
To the River Arun

On thy wild banks, by frequent torrents worn,
    No glittering fanes, or marble domes appear,
Yet shall the mournful Muse thy course adorn,
    And still to her thy rustic waves be dear.
For with the infant Otway, lingering here,   5
    Of early woes she bade her votary dream,
While thy low murmurs soothed his pensive ear,
    And still the poet consecrates the stream.
Beneath the oak and birch that fringe thy side,
    The first-born violets of the year shall spring;   10
And in thy hazels, bending o'er the tide,
    The earliest nightingale delight to sing:
While kindred spirits, pitying, shall relate
Thy Otway's sorrows, and lament his fate!

XXVII

Sighing I see yon little troop at play,
 By sorrow yet untouched; unhurt by care;
While free and sportive they enjoy today,
 'Content and careless of tomorrow's fare!'
O happy age! when hope's unclouded ray   5
 Lights their green path, and prompts their simple mirth,
Ere yet they feel the thorns that lurking lay
 To wound the wretched pilgrims of the earth,
Making them rue the hour that gave them birth,
 And threw them on a world so full of pain,   10
Where prosperous folly treads on patient worth,
 And, to deaf pride, misfortune pleads in vain!
Ah! – for their future fate how many fears
Oppress my heart – and fill mine eyes with tears!

XXXI
Written in Farm Wood, South Downs, in May 1784

Spring's dewy hand on this fair summit weaves
 The downy grass, with tufts of Alpine flowers,
And shades the beechen slopes with tender leaves,
 And leads the shepherd to his upland bowers,
Strewn with wild thyme; while slow-descending showers 5
 Feed the green ear, and nurse the future sheaves!
 Ah! blest the hind – whom no sad thought bereaves
Of the gay season's pleasures! – all his hours
To wholesome labour given, or thoughtless mirth;
 No pangs of sorrow past, or coming dread,   10
Bend his unconscious spirit down to earth,
 Or chase calm slumbers from his careless head!
Ah! what to me can those dear days restore,
When scenes could charm that now I taste no more!

XXXVI

Should the lone wanderer, fainting on his way,
    Rest for a moment of the sultry hours,
And though his path through thorns and roughness lay,
    Pluck the wild rose, or woodbine's gadding flowers,
Weaving gay wreaths beneath some sheltering tree,   5
    The sense of sorrow he awhile may lose;
So have I sought thy flowers, fair poesy!
    So charmed my way with friendship and the Muse.
But darker now grows life's unhappy day,
    Dark with new clouds of evil yet to come,   10
Her pencil sickening Fancy throws away,
    And weary Hope reclines upon the tomb;
And points my wishes to that tranquil shore,
Where the pale spectre Care pursues no more.

XL

Far on the sands, the low, retiring tide,
    In distant murmurs hardly seems to flow;
And o'er the world of waters, blue and wide,
    The sighing summer wind forgets to blow.
As sinks the day-star in the rosy west,   5
    The silent wave, with rich reflection glows:
Alas! can tranquil nature give *me* rest,
    Or scenes of beauty sooth me to repose?
Can the soft lustre of the sleeping main,
    Yon radiant heaven, or all creation's charms,   10
'Erase the written troubles of the brain',
    Which memory tortures, and which guilt alarms?
Or bid a bosom transient quiet prove,
That bleeds with vain remorse and unextinguished love!

XLIV
Written in the Churchyard at Middleton in Sussex

Pressed by the moon, mute arbitress of tides,
    While the loud equinox its power combines,
    The sea no more its swelling surge confines,
But o'er the shrinking land sublimely rides.
The wild blast, rising from the western cave,   5
    Drives the huge billows from their heaving bed;
    Tears from their grassy tombs the village dead,
And breaks the silent sabbath of the grave!
With shells and seaweed mingled, on the shore
    Lo! their bones whiten in the frequent wave;   10
    But vain to them the winds and waters rave;
They hear the warring elements no more:
While I am doomed – by life's long storm opprest,
To gaze with envy on their gloomy rest.

XLIX
Supposed to have been Written in a Churchyard, Over the Grave of a Young Woman of Nineteen

O thou! who sleep'st where hazel-bands entwine
    The vernal grass, with paler violets drest;
I would, sweet maid! thy humble bed were mine,
    And mine thy calm and enviable rest.
For never more by human ills opprest   5
    Shall thy soft spirit fruitlessly repine:
    Thou canst not now thy fondest hopes resign
Even in the hour that should have made thee blest.
Light lies the turf upon thy virgin breast;
    And lingering here, to love and sorrow true,   10
The youth who once thy simple heart possest
    Shall mingle tears with April's early dew;
While still for him shall faithful memory save
Thy form and virtues from the silent grave.

LI
Supposed to have been Written in the Hebrides

On this lone island, whose unfruitful breast
    Feeds but the summer-shepherd's little flock
    With scanty herbage from the half-clothed rock,
Where ospreys, cormorants, and sea-mews rest;
    Even in a scene so desolate and rude   5
I could with *thee* for months and years be blest;
And of thy tenderness and love possest,
    Find all *my* world in this wild solitude!
When summer suns these northern seas illume,
    With thee admire the light's reflected charms,   10
And when drear winter spreads his cheerless gloom,
    Still find Elysium in thy shelt'ring arms:
For thou to me canst sovereign bliss impart,
Thy mind my empire – and my throne thy heart.

LVIII
The Glow-Worm

When on some balmy-breathing night of spring
    The happy child, to whom the world is new,
Pursues the evening moth, of mealy wing,
    Or from the heath-bell beats the sparkling dew;
He sees before his inexperienced eyes   5
    The brilliant glow-worm, like a meteor, shine
On the turf-bank; amazed, and pleased, he cries,
    'Star of the dewy grass! – I make thee mine!' –
Then, ere he sleep, collects 'the moistened' flower,
    And bids soft leaves his glittering prize enfold,   10
And dreams that fairy-lamps illume his bower:
    Yet with the morning shudders to behold
His lucid treasure, rayless as the dust!
– So turn the world's bright joys to cold and blank disgust.

LXVI
Written in a Tempestuous Night, on the Coast of Sussex

The night-flood rakes upon the stony shore;
    Along the rugged cliffs and chalky caves
Mourns the hoarse ocean, seeming to deplore
    All that are buried in his restless waves –
Mined by corrosive tides, the hollow rock   5
    Falls prone, and rushing from its turfy height,
Shakes the broad beach with long-resounding shock,
    Loud thundering on the ear of sullen night;
Above the desolate and stormy deep,
    Gleams the wan moon, by floating mist opprest;   10
Yet here while youth, and health, and labour sleep,
    Alone I wander – calm untroubled rest,
    'Nature's soft nurse', deserts the sigh-swol'n breast,
And shuns the eyes, that only wake to weep!

LXVII
On Passing over a Dreary Tract of Country, and near the Ruins of a Deserted Chapel, During a Tempest

Swift fleet the billowy clouds along the sky,
    Earth seems to shudder at the storm aghast;
While only beings as forlorn as I,
    Court the chill horrors of the howling blast.
Even round yon crumbling walls, in search of food,   5
    The ravenous owl foregoes his evening flight,
And in his cave, within the deepest wood,
    The fox eludes the tempest of the night.
But to *my* heart congenial is the gloom
    Which hides me from a world I wish to shun;   10
That scene where ruin saps the mouldering tomb,
    Suits with the sadness of a wretch undone.
Nor is the deepest shade, the keenest air,
Black as my fate, or cold as my despair.

LXXI
Written at Weymouth in Winter

The chill waves whiten in the sharp north-east;
  Cold, cold the night-blast comes, with sullen sound;
And black and gloomy, like my cheerless breast,
  Frowns the dark pier and lonely sea-view round.
Yet a few months – and on the peopled strand   5
  Pleasure shall all her varied forms display;
Nymphs lightly tread the bright reflecting sand,
  And proud sails whiten all the summer bay:
Then, for these winds that whistle keen and bleak,
  Music's delightful melodies shall float   10
O'er the blue waters; but 'tis mine to seek
  Rather, some unfrequented shade, remote
From sights and sounds of gaiety – I mourn
All that gave *me* delight – Ah! never to return!

LXXV

Where the wild woods and pathless forests frown,
  The darkling pilgrim seeks his unknown way,
Till on the grass he throws him weary down,
  To wait in broken sleep the dawn of day:
Thro' boughs just waving in the silent air,   5
  With pale capricious light the summer moon
Chequers his humid couch; while Fancy there,
  That loves to wanton in the night's deep noon,
Calls from the mossy roots and fountain edge
  Fair visionary nymphs that haunt the shade,   10
Or naiads rising from the whispering sedge;
  And, 'mid the beauteous group, his dear loved maid
Seems beckoning him with smiles to join the train:
Then, starting from his dream, he feels his woes again!

LXXVII
To the Insect of the Gossamer

Small, viewless æronaut, that by the line
    Of gossamer suspended, in mid air
    Float'st on a sunbeam – living atom, where
Ends thy breeze-guided voyage; with what design
    In æther dost thou launch thy form minute,   5
Mocking the eye? – Alas! before the veil
    Of denser clouds shall hide thee, the pursuit
Of the keen swift may end thy fairy sail!
    Thus on the golden thread that Fancy weaves
Buoyant, as Hope's illusive flattery breathes,   10
    The young and visionary poet leaves
Life's dull realities, while sevenfold wreaths
    Of rainbow-light around his head revolve.
    Ah! soon at Sorrow's touch the radiant dreams dissolve!

LXXVIII
Snowdrops

Wan heralds of the sun and summer gale!
    That seem just fallen from infant zephyrs' wing;
Not now, as once, with heart revived I hail
    Your modest buds, that for the brow of spring
Form the first simple garland. Now no more   5
    Escaping for a moment all my cares,
Shall I, with pensive, silent step, explore
    The woods yet leafless; where to chilling airs
Your green and pencilled blossoms, trembling, wave.
    Ah! ye soft, transient children of the ground,   10
More fair was she on whose untimely grave
    Flow my unceasing tears! Their varied round
The seasons go; while I through all repine:
For fixed regret, and hopeless grief are mine.

LXXIX
To the Goddess of Botany

Of folly weary, shrinking from the view
    Of violence and fraud, allowed to take
    All peace from humble life; I would forsake
Their haunts for ever, and, sweet nymph! with you
    Find shelter; where my tired, and tear-swol'n eyes,   5
Among your silent shades of soothing hue,
    Your 'bells and florets of unnumbered dyes'
    Might rest – and learn the bright varieties
That from your lovely hands are fed with dew;
    And every veined leaf, that trembling sighs   10
In mead or woodland; or in wilds remote,
    Or lurk with mosses in the humid caves,
Mantle the cliffs, on dimpling rivers float,
    Or stream from coral rocks beneath the ocean waves.

LXXXI

He may be envied, who with tranquil breast
    Can wander in the wild and woodland scene,
When summer's glowing hands have newly drest
    The shadowy forests, and the copses green;
Who, unpursued by care, can pass his hours   5
    Where briony and woodbine fringe the trees,
    On thymy banks reposing, while the bees
Murmur 'their fairy tunes in praise of flowers';
    Or on the rock with ivy clad, and fern
That overhangs the osier-whispering bed   10
    Of some clear current, bid his wishes turn
From this bad world; and by calm reason led,
    Knows, in refined retirement, to possess
    By friendship hallowed – rural happiness!

LXXXVI
Written near a Port on a Dark Evening

Huge vapours brood above the clifted shore,
    Night on the ocean settles, dark and mute,
Save where is heard the repercussive roar
    Of drowsy billows, on the rugged foot
Or rocks remote; or still more distant tone   5
    Of seamen in the anchored bark that tell
The watch relieved; or one deep voice alone
    Singing the hour, and bidding 'Strike the bell',
All is black shadow, but the lucid line
    Marked by the light surf on the level sand,   10
Or where afar the ship-lights faintly shine
    Like wandering fairy fires, that oft on land
Mislead the pilgrim – such the dubious ray
That wavering reason lends, in life's long darkling way.

LXXXVII
Written in October

The blasts of autumn as they scatter round
    The faded foliage of another year,
And muttering many a sad and solemn sound,
    Drive the pale fragments o'er the stubble sere,
Are well attuned to my dejected mood;   5
    (Ah! better far than airs that breathe of spring!)
    While the high rooks, that hoarsely clamouring
Seek in black phalanx the half-leafless wood,
    I rather hear, than that enraptured lay
Harmonious, and of love and pleasure born,   10
Which from the golden furze, or flowering thorn
    Awakes the shepherd in the ides of May;
Nature delights me most when most she mourns,
For never more to me the spring of hope returns!

XCI
Reflections on Some Drawings of Plants

I can in groups these mimic flowers compose,
    These bells and golden eyes, embathed in dew;
Catch the soft blush that warms the early rose,
    Or the pale iris cloud with veins of blue;
Copy the scalloped leaves, and downy stems,   5
    And bid the pencil's varied shades arrest
Spring's humid buds, and summer's musky gems:
    But, save the portrait on my bleeding breast,
I have no semblance of that form adored,
    That form, expressive of a soul divine,   10
    So early blighted; and while life is mine,
With fond regret, and ceaseless grief deplored –
    That grief, my angel! with too faithful art
    Enshrines thy image in thy mother's heart.

Thirty-Eight
Addressed to Mrs H——Y

In early youth's unclouded scene,
The brilliant morning of eighteen,
With health and sprightly joy elate
    We gazed on life's enchanting spring,
    Nor thought how quickly time would bring   5
The mournful period – thirty-eight.

Then the starch maid, or matron sage,
Already of that sober age,
We viewed with mingled scorn and hate;
    In whose sharp words, or sharper face,   10
    With thoughtless mirth we loved to trace
The sad effects of – thirty-eight.

Till saddening, sickening at the view,
We learned to dread what time might do;
And then preferred a prayer to fate   15
  To end our days ere that arrived;
  When (power and pleasure long survived)
We met neglect and – thirty-eight.

But time, in spite of wishes flies,
And fate our simple prayer denies,   20
And bids us death's own hour await:
  The auburn locks are mixed with grey,
  The transient roses fade away,
But reason comes at – thirty-eight.

Her voice the anguish contradicts   25
That dying vanity inflicts;
Her hand new pleasures can create,
  For us she opens to the view
  Prospects less bright – but far more true,
And bids us smile at – thirty-eight.   30

No more shall scandal's breath destroy
The social converse we enjoy
With bard or critic tête à tête;
  O'er youth's bright blooms her blights shall pour,
  But spare the improving friendly hour   35
That science gives to – thirty-eight.

Stripped of their gaudy hues by truth,
We view the glitt'ring toys of youth,
And blush to think how poor the bait
  For which to public scenes we ran   40
  And scorned of sober sense the plan
Which gives content at – thirty-eight.

Tho' time's inexorable sway
Has torn the myrtle bands away,
For other wreaths 'tis not too late,   45
  The amaranth's purple glow survives,
  And still Minerva's olive lives
On the calm brow of – thirty-eight.

15

With eye more steady we engage
To contemplate approaching age, 50
And life more justly estimate;
    With firmer souls, and stronger powers,
    With reason, faith, and friendship ours,
    We'll not regret the stealing hours
That lead from thirty – even to forty-eight. 55

Verses Supposed to Have Been Written in the New Forest, in Early Spring

As in the woods, where leathery lichen weaves
Its wintry web among the sallow leaves,
Which (thro' cold months in whirling eddies blown)
Decay beneath the branches once their own,
From the brown shelter of their foliage sear, 5
Spring the young blooms that lead the floral year:
When, waked by vernal suns, the pilewort dares
Expand her spotted leaves, and shining stars;
And (veins empurpling all her tassels pale)
Bends the soft windflower in the tepid gale; 10
Uncultured bells of azure jacinths blow,
And the breeze-scenting violet lurks below;
So views the wanderer, with delighted eyes,
Reviving hopes from black despondence rise,
When, blighted by Adversity's chill breath, 15
Those hopes that felt a temporary death;
Then with gay heart he looks to future hours,
When Love shall dress him for the summer bowers!
And, as delicious dreams enchant his mind,
Forgets his sorrows past, or gives them to the wind. 20

The Forest Boy

The trees have now hid at the edge of the hurst
    The spot where the ruins decay
Of the cottage, where Will of the Woodlands was nursed
And lived so beloved, till the moment accurst
    When he went from the woodland away.   5

Among all the lads of the plough or the fold,
    Best esteemed by the sober and good,
Was Will of the Woodlands; and often the old
Would tell of his frolics, for active and bold
    Was William the boy of the wood.   10

Yet gentle was he, as the breath of the May,
    And when sick and declining was laid
The woodman his father, young William away
Would go to the forest to labour all day,
    And perform his hard task in his stead.   15

And when his poor father the forester died,
    And his mother was sad, and alone,
He toiled from the dawn, and at evening he hied
In storm or in snow, or whate'er might betide,
    To supply all her wants from the town.   20

One neighbour they had on the heath to the west,
    And no other the cottage was near,
But she would send Phoebe, the child she loved best,
To stay with the widow, thus sad and distrest,
    Her hours of dejection to cheer.   25

As the buds of wild roses, the cheeks of the maid
    Were just tinted with youth's lovely hue,
Her form like the aspen, soft graces displayed,
And the eyes, over which her luxuriant locks strayed,
    As the skies of the summer were blue!   30

Still labouring to live, yet reflecting the while,
    Young William considered his lot;
'Twas hard, yet 'twas honest; and one tender smile
From Phoebe at night overpaid ev'ry toil,
    And then all his fatigues were forgot.   35

By the brook where it glides thro' the copse of Arbeal,
    When to eat his cold fare he reclined,
Then soft from her home his sweet Phoebe would steal
And bring him wood-strawberries to finish his meal,
    And would sit by his side while he dined.   40

And tho' when employed in the deep forest glade,
    His days have seemed slowly to move,
Yet Phoebe going home, thro' the wood-walk has strayed
To bid him goodnight! – and whatever she said
    Was more sweet than the voice of the dove.   45

Fair hope, that the lover so fondly believes,
    Then repeated each soul-soothing speech,
And touched with illusion, that often deceives
The future with light; as the sun thro' the leaves
    Illumines the boughs of the beech.   50

But once more the tempests of chill winter blow,
    To depress and disfigure the earth;
And now ere the dawn, the young woodman must go
To his work in the forest, half buried in snow,
    And at night bring home wood for the hearth.   55

The bridge on the heath by the flood was washed down,
    And fast, fast fell the sleet and the rain,
The stream to a wild rapid river was grown,
And long might the widow sit sighing alone
    Ere sweet Phoebe could see her again.   60

At the town was a market – and now for supplies
    Such as needed their humble abode,
Young William went forth; and his mother with sighs
Watched long at the window, with tears in her eyes,
    Till he turned thro' the fields, to the road.   65

Then darkness came on; and she heard with affright
    The wind rise every moment more high;
She looked from the door; not a star lent its light,
But the tempest redoubled the gloom of the night,
    And the rain fell in floods from the sky.   70

The clock in her cottage now mournfully told
    The hours that went heavily on;
'Twas midnight; her spirits sunk hopeless and cold,
For the wind seemed to say as in loud gusts it rolled,
    That long, long would her William be gone.   75

Then heart-sick and faint to her sad bed she crept,
    Yet first made up the fire in the room
To guide his dark steps; but she listened and wept,
Or if for a moment forgetful she slept,
    She soon started! – and thought he was come.   80

'Twas morn; and the wind with an hoarse sullen moan
    Now seemed dying away in the wood,
When the poor wretched mother still drooping, alone,
Beheld on the threshold a figure unknown,
    In gorgeous apparel who stood.   85

'Your son is a soldier,' abruptly cried he,
    'And a place in our corps has obtained,
Nay, be not cast down; you perhaps may soon see
Your William a captain! He now sends by me
    The purse he already has gained.'   90

So William entrapped 'twixt persuasion and force,
    Is embarked for the Isles of the West,
But he seemed to begin with ill omens his course,
And felt recollection, regret, and remorse
    Continually weigh on his breast.   95

With useless repentance he eagerly eyed
    The high coast as it faded from view,
And saw the green hills, on whose northernmost side
Was his own sylvan home: and he faltered and cried
    'Adieu! Ah! for ever adieu!   100

19

'Who now, my poor mother, thy life shall sustain,
    Since thy son has thus left thee forlorn?
Ah! canst thou forgive me? And not in the pain
Of this cruel desertion, of William complain,
    And lament that he ever was born?   105

'Sweet Phoebe! – if ever thy lover was dear,
    Now forsake not the cottage of woe,
But comfort my mother; and quiet her fear,
And help her to dry up the vain fruitless tear
    That too long for my absence will flow.   110

'Yet what if my Phoebe another should wed,
    And lament her lost William no more?'
The thought was too cruel; and anguish soon sped
The dart of disease – with the brave numerous dead
    He has fall'n on the plague-tainted shore.   115

In the lone village churchyard, the chancel-wall near,
    The high grass now waves over the spot
Where the mother of William, unable to bear
His loss, who to her widowed heart was so dear,
    Has both him and her sorrows forgot.   120

By the brook where it winds thro' the wood of Arbeal,
    Or amid the deep forest, to moan,
The poor wandering Phoebe will silently steal;
The pain of her bosom no reason can heal,
    And she loves to indulge it alone.   125

Her senses are injured; her eyes dim with tears;
    By the river she ponders; and weaves
Reed garlands, against her dear William appears,
Then breathlessly listens, and fancies she hears
    His light step in the half-withered leaves.   130

Ah! such are the miseries to which ye give birth,
    Ye cold statesmen! Unknowing a scar;
Who from pictured saloon, or the bright sculptured hearth,
Disperse desolation and death thro' the earth,
    When ye let loose the demons of war.   135

From *The Emigrants*

Book the First

SCENE, on the cliffs to the eastward of the town of Brighthelmstone
   in Sussex.
TIME, a morning in November, 1792.

Slow in the wintry morn, the struggling light
Throws a faint gleam upon the troubled waves;
Their foaming tops, as they approach the shore
And the broad surf that never ceasing breaks
On the innumerous pebbles, catch the beams   5
Of the pale sun, that with reluctance gives
To this cold northern isle, its shortened day.
Alas! how few the morning wakes to joy!
How many murmur at oblivious night
For leaving them so soon; for bearing thus   10
Their fancied bliss (the only bliss they taste!),
On her black wings away! Changing the dreams
That soothed their sorrows, for calamities
(And every day brings its own sad proportion)
For doubts, diseases, abject dread of death,   15
And faithless friends, and fame and fortune lost;
Fancied or real wants; and wounded pride,
That views the day star, but to curse his beams.
Yet he, whose spirit into being called
This wond'rous world of waters; he who bids   20
The wild wind lift them till they dash the clouds,
And speaks to them in thunder; or whose breath,
Low murmuring o'er the gently heaving tides,
When the fair moon, in summer night serene,
Irradiates with long trembling lines of light   25
Their undulating surface; that great power,
Who, governing the planets, also knows
If but a sea-mew falls, whose nest is hid
In these incumbent cliffs; he surely means
To us, his reasoning creatures, whom he bids   30
Acknowledge and revere his awful hand,
Nothing but good: yet man, misguided man,

Mars the fair work that he was bid enjoy,
And makes himself the evil he deplores.
How often, when my weary soul recoils   35
From proud oppression, and from legal crimes
(For such are in this land, where the vain boast
Of equal law is mockery, while the cost
Of seeking for redress is sure to plunge
Th'already injured to more certain ruin   40
And the wretch starves, before his counsel pleads)
How often do I half abjure society,
And sigh for some lone cottage, deep embowered
In the green woods, that these steep chalky hills
Guard from the strong south west; where round their base 45
The beach wide flourishes, and the light ash
With slender leaf half hides the thymy turf!
There do I wish to hide me; well content
If on the short grass, strewn with fairy flowers,
I might repose thus sheltered; or when eve   50
In orient crimson lingers in the west,
Gain the high mound, and mark these waves remote
(Lucid tho' distant), blushing with the rays
Of the far-flaming orb, that sinks beneath them;
For I have thought, that I should then behold   55
The beauteous works of God, unspoiled by man
And less affected then, by human woes
I witnessed not; might better learn to bear
Those that injustice, and duplicity
And faithlessness and folly, fix on me: 60
For never yet could I derive relief,
When my swol'n heart was bursting with its sorrows,
From the sad thought, that others like myself
Live but to swell affliction's countless tribes!
Tranquil seclusion I have vainly sought;   65
Peace, who delights in solitary shade,
No more will spread for me her downy wings,
But, like the fabled Danaïds – or the wretch,
Who ceaseless, up the steep acclivity,
Was doomed to heave the still rebounding rock,   70
Onward I labour; as the baffled wave,
Which yon rough beach repulses, that returns
With the next breath of wind, to fail again.

Ah! mourner – cease these wailings: cease and learn,
That not the cot sequestered, where the briar   75
And woodbine wild, embrace the mossy thatch,
(Scarce seen amid the forest gloom obscure!)
Or more substantial farm, well fenced and warm,
Where the full barn, and cattle foddered round
Speak rustic plenty; nor the statelier dome   80
By dark firs shaded, or the aspiring pine,
Close by the village church (with care concealed
By verdant foliage, lest the poor man's grave
Should mar the smiling prospect of his lord),
Where offices well-ranged, or dovecote stocked,   85
Declare manorial residence; not these
Or any of the buildings, new and trim
With windows circling towards the restless sea,
Which ranged in rows, now terminate my walk,
Can shut out for an hour the spectre care,   90
That from the dawn of reason, follows still
Unhappy mortals, 'till the friendly grave
(Our sole secure asylum) 'ends the chase'.

*

Where the cliff, hollowed by the wintry storm,   200
Affords a seat with matted seaweed strewn,
A softer form reclines; around her run,
On the rough shingles, or the chalky bourn,
Her gay unconscious children, soon amused;
Who pick the fretted stone, or glossy shell,   205
Or crimson plant marine: or they contrive
The fairy vessel, with its ribbon sail
And gilded paper pennant: in the pool,
Left by the salt wave on the yielding sands,
They launch the mimic navy – happy age!   210
Unmindful of the miseries of man!
Alas! too long a victim to distress,
Their mother, lost in melancholy thought,
Lulled for a moment by the murmurs low
Of sullen billows, wearied by the task   215
Of having here, with swol'n and aching eyes
Fixed on the grey horizon, since the dawn

Solicitously watched the weekly sail
From her dear native land, now yields awhile
To kind forgetfulness, while Fancy brings,   220
In waking dreams, that native land again!
Versailles appears — its painted galleries,
And rooms of regal splendour, rich with gold,
Where, by long mirrors multiplied, the crowd
Paid willing homage — and, united there,   225
Beauty gave charms to empire. Ah! too soon
From the gay visionary pageant roused,
See the sad mourner start! — and, drooping, look
With tearful eyes and heaving bosom round
On drear reality — where dark'ning waves,   230
Urged by the rising wind, unheeded foam
Near her cold rugged seat. To call her thence
A fellow-sufferer comes: dejection deep
Checks, but conceals not quite, the martial air,
And that high consciousness of noble blood,   235
Which he has learned from infancy to think
Exalts him o'er the race of common men:
Nursed in the velvet lap of luxury,
And fed by adulation — could *he* learn,
That worth alone is true nobility?   240

                          *

               As one, who long   260
Has dwelt amid the artificial scenes
Of populous city, deems that splendid shows,
The theatre, and pageant pomp of courts,
Are only worth regard; forgets all taste
For nature's genuine beauty; in the lapse   265
Of gushing waters hears no soothing sound,
Nor listens with delight to sighing winds,
That, on their fragrant pinions, waft the notes
Of birds rejoicing in the trangled copse;
Nor gazes pleased on ocean's silver breast,   270
While lightly o'er it sails the summer clouds
Reflected in the wave, that, hardly heard,
Flows on the yellow sands: so to his mind,
That long has lived where despotism hides

His features harsh, beneath the diadem 275
Of worldly grandeur, abject slavery seems,
If by that power imposed, slavery no more:
For luxury wreathes with silk the iron bonds,
And hides the ugly rivets with her flowers,
Till the degenerate triflers, while they love 280
The glitter of the chains, forget their weight.

*

Poor wand'ring wretches! Whosoe'er ye are,
That hopeless, houseless, friendless, travel wide
O'er these bleak russet downs; where, dimly seen,
The solitary shepherd shiv'ring tends
His dun discoloured flock (shepherd, unlike 300
Him, whom in song the poet's fancy crowns
With garlands, and his crook with violets binds);
Poor vagrant wretches! Outcasts of the world!
Whom no abode receives, no parish owns;
Roving, like nature's commoners, the land 305
That boasts such general plenty: if the sight
Of wide-extended misery softens yours
Awhile, suspend your murmurs! Here behold
The strange vicissitudes of fate – while thus
The exiled nobles, from their country driven, 310
Whose richest luxuries were theirs, must feel
More poignant anguish, than the lowest poor,
Who, born to indigence, have learned to brave
Rigid Adversity's depressing breath!
Ah! rather Fortune's worthless favourites! 315
Who feed on England's vitals – pensioners
Of base corruption, who, in quick ascent
To opulence unmerited, become
Giddy with pride, and as ye rise, forgetting
The dust ye lately left, with scorn look down 320
On those beneath ye (tho' your equals once
In fortune, and in worth superior still,
They view the eminence, on which ye stand,
With wonder, not with envy; for they know
The means, by which ye reached it, have been such 325
As, in all honest eyes, degrade ye far

25

Beneath the poor dependant, whose sad heart
Reluctant pleads for what your pride denies);
Ye venal, worthless hirelings of a court!
Ye pampered parasites! Whom Britons pay   330
For forging fetters for them, rather here
Study a lesson that concerns ye much;
And, trembling, learn, that if oppressed too long,
The raging multitude, to madness stung,
Will turn on their oppressors; and, no more   335
By sounding titles and parading forms
Bound like tame victims, will redress themselves!

Book the Second

SCENE, on an eminence on one of those Downs, which afford to the
        south a view of the sea; to the north of the Weald of Sussex.
TIME, an afternoon in April, 1793.

Long wintry months are past; the moon that now
Lights her pale crescent even at noon, has made
Four times her revolution; since with step,
Mournful and slow, along the wave-worn cliff,
Pensive I took my solitary way,   5
Lost in despondence, while contemplating
Not my own wayward destiny alone,
(Hard as it is, and difficult to bear!)
But in beholding the unhappy lot
Of the lorn exiles; who, amid the storms   10
Of wild disastrous anarchy, are thrown,
Like shipwrecked sufferers, on England's coast,
To see, perhaps, no more their native land,
Where desolation riots: they, like me,
From fairer hopes and happier prospects driven,   15
Shrink from the future, and regret the past.
But on this upland scene, while April comes,
With fragrant airs, to fan my throbbing breast,
Fain would I snatch an interval from care,
That weighs my wearied spirit down to earth;   20
Courting, once more, the influence of hope
(For hope still waits upon the flowery prime)

As here I mark spring's humid hand unfold
The early leaves that fear capricious winds,
While, even on sheltered banks, the timid flowers   25
Give, half reluctantly, their warmer hues
To mingle with the primroses' pale stars.
No shade the leafless copses yet afford,
Nor hide the mossy labours of the thrush,
That, startled, darts across the narrow path;   30
But quickly reassured, resumes his task,
Or adds his louder notes to those that rise
From yonder tufted brake; where the white buds
Of the first thorn are mingled with the leaves
Of that which blossoms on the brow of May.   35
Ah! 'twill not be – so many years have passed,
Since, on my native hills, I learned to gaze
On these delightful landscapes; and those years
Have taught me so much sorrow, that my soul
Feels not the joy reviving nature brings;   40
But, in dark retrospect, dejected dwells
On human follies, and on human woes.
What is the promise of the infant year,
The lively verdure, or the bursting blooms,
To those, who shrink from horrors such as war   45
Spreads o'er the affrighted world? With swimming eye,
Back on the past they throw their mournful looks,
And see the temple, which they fondly hoped
Reason would raise to liberty, destroyed
By ruffian hands; while, on the ruined mass,   50
Flushed with hot blood, the Fiend of Discord sits
In savage triumph; mocking every plea
Of policy and justice, as she shows
The headless corse of one whose only crime
Was being born a monarch – Mercy turns,   55
From spectacle so dire, her swol'n eyes;
And Liberty, with calm, unruffled brow
Magnanimous, as conscious of her strength
In Reason's panoply, scorns to distain
Her righteous cause with carnage, and resigns   60
To Fraud and Anarchy the infuriate crowd.

*

27

Alas! in rural life, where youthful dreams
See the Arcadia that Romance describes,
Not even Content resides! In yon low hut   180
Of clay and thatch, where rises the grey smoke
Of smold'ring turf, cut from the adjoining moor,
The labourer, its inhabitant, who toils
From the first dawn of twilight, till the sun
Sinks in the rosy waters of the west,   185
Finds that with poverty it cannot dwell;
For bread, and scanty bread, is all he earns
For him and for his household – should Disease,
Born of chill wintry rains, arrest his arm,
Then, thro' his patched and straw-stuffed casement, peeps   190
The squalid figure of extremest Want;
And from the parish the reluctant dole,
Dealt by th'unfeeling farmer, hardly saves
The ling'ring spark of life from cold extinction:
Then the bright sun of spring, that smiling bids   195
All other animals rejoice, beholds,
Crept from his pallet, the emaciate wretch
Attempt, with feeble effort, to resume
Some heavy task, above his wasted strength,
Turning his wistful looks (how much in vain!)   200
To the deserted mansion, where no more
The owner (gone to gayer scenes) resides,
Who made even luxury, virtue; while he gave
The scattered crumbs to honest poverty.
But, tho' the landscape be too oft deformed   205
By figures such as these, yet peace is here,
And o'er our valleys, clothed with springing corn,
No hostile hoof shall trample, nor fierce flames
Wither the wood's young verdure, ere it form
Gradual the laughing May's luxuriant shade;   210
For, by the rude sea guarded, we are safe,
And feel not evils such as with deep sighs
The emigrants deplore, as they recall
The summer past, when nature seemed to lose
Her course in wild distemperature, and aid,   215
With seasons all reversed, destructive war.

*

The feudal chief, whose Gothic battlements
Frown on the plain beneath, returning home
From distant lands, alone and in disguise,   295
Gains at the fall of night his castle walls,
But, at the vacant gate, no porter sits
To wait his lord's admittance! In the courts
All is drear silence! Guessing but too well
The fatal truth, he shudders as he goes   300
Thro' the mute hall; where, by the blunted light
That the dim moon thro' painted casements lends,
He sees that devastation has been there:
Then, while each hideous image to his mind
Rises terrific, o'er a bleeding corse   305
Stumbling he falls; another interrupts
His staggering feet – all, all who used to rush
With joy to meet him – all his family
Lie murdered in his way! And the day dawns
On a wild raving maniac, whom a fate   310
So sudden and calamitous has robbed
Of reason; and who round his vacant walls
Screams unregarded, and reproaches heaven!
Such are thy dreadful trophies, savage war!

*

          Memory come!
And from distracting cares, that now deprive   330
Such scenes of all their beauty, kindly bear
My fancy to those hours of simple joy,
When, on the banks of Arun, which I see
Make its irriguous course thro' yonder meads,
I played; unconscious then of future ill!   335
There (where, from hollows fringed with yellow broom,
The birch with silver rind, and fairy leaf,
Aslant the low stream trembles) I have stood,
And meditated how to venture best
Into the shallow current, to procure   340
The willowherb of glowing purple spikes,
Or flags, whose sword-like leaves concealed the tide,
Startling the timid reed-bird from her nest,
As with aquatic flowers I wove the wreath,

Such as, collected by the shepherd girls,   345
Deck in the villages the turfy shrine,
And mark the arrival of propitious May.
How little dreamed I then the time would come,
When the bright sun of that delicious month
Should, from disturbed and artificial sleep,   350
Awaken me to neverending toil,
To terror and to tears! Attempting still,
With feeble hands and cold desponding heart,
To save my children from the o'erwhelming wrongs,
That have for ten long years been heaped on me!   355
The fearful spectres of chicane and fraud
Have, Proteus-like, still changed their hideous forms
(As the law lent its plausible disguise),
Pursuing my faint steps; and I have seen
Friendship's sweet bonds (which were so early formed,   360
And once I fondly thought of amaranth
Inwove with silver seven times tried) give way,
And fail; as these green fan-like leaves of fern
Will wither at the touch of autumn's frost.
Yet there are those, whose patient pity still   365
Hears my long murmurs; who, unwearied, try
With lenient hands to bind up every wound
My wearied spirit feels, and bid me go
'Right onward' – a calm votary of the nymph,
Who, from her adamantine rock, points out   370
To conscious rectitude the rugged path,
That leads at length to peace! Ah! yes, my friends
Peace will at last be mine; for in the grave
Is peace – and pass a few short years, perchance
A few short months, and all the various pain   375
I now endure shall be forgotten there,
And no memorial shall remain of me,
Save in your bosoms; while even your regret
Shall lose its poignancy, as ye reflect
What complicated woes that grave conceals!   380

From *Conversations Introducing Poetry; Chiefly on Subjects of Natural History, For the Use of Children and Young Persons*

A Walk by the Water

Let us walk where reeds are growing,
    By the alders in the mead;
Where the crystal streams are flowing,
    In whose waves the fishes feed.

There the golden carp is laving,   5
    With the trout, the perch, and bream;
Mark! Their flexile fins are waving,
    As they glance along the stream.

Now they sink in deeper billows,
    Now upon the surface rise;   10
Or from under roots of willows,
    Dart to catch the water flies.

'Midst the reeds and pebbles hiding,
    See the minnow and the roach;
Or by waterlilies gliding,   15
    Shun with fear our near approach.

Do not dread us timid fishes,
    We have neither net nor hook;
Wanderers we, whose only wishes
    Are to read in nature's book.   20

The Hedgehog Seen in a Frequented Path

Wherefore should man or thoughtless boy
Thy quiet harmless life destroy,
Innoxious urchin? For thy food
Is but the beetle and the fly,
And all thy harmless luxury   5
The swarming insects of the wood.

Should man to whom his God has given
Reason, the brightest ray of heaven,
Delight to hurt, in senseless mirth,
Inferior animals? – and dare   10
To use his power in waging war
Against his brethren of the earth?

Poor creature! To the woods resort,
Lest lingering here, inhuman sport
Should render vain thy thorny case;   15
And whelming water, deep and cold,
Make thee thy spiny ball unfold,
And show thy simple negro face!

Fly from the cruel; know than they
Less fierce are ravenous beasts of prey,   20
And should perchance these last come near thee;
And fox or martin cat assail,
Thou, safe within thy coat of mail,
May cry – Ah! *noli me tangere*.

The Moth

When dews fall fast, and rosy day
Fades slowly in the west away,
While evening breezes bend the future sheaves;
Votary of vesper's humid light,
The moth, pale wanderer of the night,   5
From his green cradle comes, amid the whispering leaves.

The birds on insect life that feast,
Now in their woody coverts rest,
The swallow slumbers in his dome of clay,
And of the numerous tribes who war   10
On the small denizens of air,
The shrieking bat alone is on the wing for prey.

Eluding him, on lacy plume
The silver moth enjoys the gloom,
Glancing on tremulous wing thro' twilight bowers,   15
Now flits where warm nasturtiums glow,
Now quivers on the jasmine bough,
And sucks with spiral tongue the balm of sleeping flowers.

Yet if from open casement stream
The taper's bright aspiring beam,   20
And strikes with comet ray his dazzled sight;
Nor perfumed leaf, nor honeyed flower,
To check his wild career have power,
But to the attracting flame he takes his rapid flight.

Round it he darts in dizzy rings,   25
And soon his soft and powdered wings
Are singed; and dimmer grow his pearly eyes,
And now his struggling feet are foiled,
And scorched, entangled, burnt, and soiled,
His fragile form is lost – the wretched insect dies! 30

Emblem too just of one, whose way
Thro the calm vale of life might lay,
Yet lured by vanity's illusive fires
Far from that tranquil vale aside,
Like this poor insect suicide   35
Follows the fatal light, and in its flame expires.

To the Firefly of Jamaica, Seen in a Collection

How art thou altered! Since afar,
Thou seem'dst a bright earth wandering star;
When thy living lustre ran,
Tall majestic trees between,
And guazume, or swietan,   5
Or the pimento's glossy green,
As caught their varnished leaves, thy glancing light
Reflected flying fires, amid the moonless night.

From shady heights, where currents spring,
Where the ground dove dips her wing,   10
Winds of night reviving blow,
Thro' rustling fields of maize and cane,
And wave the coffee's fragrant bough;
But winds of night, for thee in vain
May breathe, of the plumeria's luscious bloom,   15
Or granate's scarlet buds, or plinia's mild perfume.

The recent captive, who in vain,
Attempts to break his heavy chain,
And find his liberty in flight;
Shall no more in terror hide,   20
From thy strange and doubtful light,
In the mountain's caverned side,
Or gully deep, where gibbering monkeys cling,
And broods the giant bat, on dark funereal wing.

Nor thee his darkling steps to aid,   25
Thro' the forest's pathless shade,
Shall the sighing slave invoke;
Who, his daily task performed,
Would forget his heavy yoke;
And by fond affections warmed,   30
Glide to some dear sequestered spot, to prove,
Friendship's consoling voice, or sympathising love.

Now, when sinks the sun away,
And fades at once the sultry day,
Thee, as falls the sudden night,   35
Never naturalist shall view,
Dart with coruscation bright,
Down the coco avenue;
Or see thee give, with transient gleams to glow,
The green banana's head, or shaddock's loaded bough.   40

Ah! never more shalt thou behold,
The midnight beauty, slow unfold
Her golden zone, and thro' the gloom
To thee her radiant leaves display,
More lovely than the roseate bloom   45
Of flowers, that drink the tropic day;
And while thy dancing flames around her blaze,
Shed odours more refined, and beam with brighter rays.

The glass thy faded form contains,
But of thy lamp no spark remains;   50
That lamp, which through the palmy grove,
Floated once with sapphire beam,
As lucid as the star of love,
Reflected in the bickering stream;
Transient and bright! So human meteors rise   55
And glare and sink, in pensive Reason's eyes.

Ye dazzling comets that appear
In fashion's rainbow atmosphere,
Lightning and flashing for a day;
Think ye, how fugitive your fame?   60
How soon from her light scroll away,
Is wafted your ephemeron name?
Even tho' on canvas still your forms are shown,
Or the slow chisel shapes the pale resembling stone.

Let vaunting ostentation trust   65
The pencil's art, or marble bust,
While long neglected modest worth,
Unmarked, unhonoured, and unknown,
Obtains at length a little earth,
Where kindred merit weeps alone;   70
Yet there, tho' vanity no trophies rear,
Is friendship's long regret, and true affection's tear!

To a Geranium which Flowered during the Winter.
Written in Autumn

Native of Afric's arid lands,
Thou, and thy many-tinctured bands,
Unheeded and unvalued grew,
While Caffres crushed beneath the sands
Thy pencilled flowers of roseate hue.   5

But our cold northern sky beneath,
For thee attempered zephyrs breathe,
And art supplies the tepid dew,
That feeds, in many a glowing wreath,
Thy lovely flowers of roseate hue.   10

Thy race, that spring uncultured here,
Decline with the declining year,
While in successive beauty new,
Thine own light bouquets fresh appear,
And marbled leaves of cheerful hue.   15

Now buds and bells of every shade,
By summer's ardent eye surveyed,
No more their gorgeous colours show;
And even the lingering asters fade,
With drooping heads of purple hue.   20

But naturalised in foreign earth,
'Tis thine, with many a beauteous birth,
As if in gratitude they blew,
To hang, like blushing trophies forth,
Thy pencilled flowers of roseate hue.   25

Oh then, amidst the wintry gloom,
Those flowers shall dress my cottage room,
Like friends in adverse fortune true;
And soothe me with their roseate bloom,
And downy leaves of vernal hue.   30

From *Beachy Head and Other Poems*

Flora

The vision comes! While slowly melt away,
Night's hovering shades before the eastern ray,
Ere yet declines the morning's humid star,
Fair Fancy brings her; in her leafy car
Flora descends, to dress the expecting earth,   25
Awake the germs, and call the buds to birth;
Bid each hybernacle its cell unfold,
And open silken leaves, and eyes of gold!

Of forest foliage of the firmest shade
Enwove by magic hands, the car was made;   30
Oak, and the ample plane, without entwined,
And beech and ash the verdant concave lined;
The saxifrage, that snowy flowers emboss,
Supplied the seat; and of the mural moss
The velvet footstool rose, where lightly rest,   35
Her slender feet in Cypripedium drest.
The tufted rush, that bears a silken crown,
The floating feathers of the thistle's down,
In tender hues of rainbow lustre dyed,
The airy texture of her robe supplied,   40
And wild convolvuli, yet half unblown,
Formed, with their wreathing buds, her simple zone,
Some wandering tresses of her radiant hair,
Luxuriant floated on the enamoured air;
The rest were by the Scandix' points confined   45
And graced a shining knot, her head behind –
While, as a sceptre of supreme command,
She waved the Anthoxanthum in her hand.

*

From depths where corals spring from crystal caves,
And break with scarlet branch, the eddying waves,   180
Where algæ stream, as change the flowing tides,

And where, half flower, half fish, the polyp hides,
And long tenacious bands of sea-lace twine
Round palm-shaped leaves impearled with coralline,
Enamoured Fancy now the sea-maids calls,   185
And from their grottos dim, and shell-paved halls,
Charmed by her voice, the shining train emerge,
And buoyant float above the circling surge;
Green byssus, waving in the sea-born gales,
Formed their thin mantles, and transparent veils,   190
Panniered in shells, or bound with silver strings,
Of silken Pinna; each her trophy brings
Of plants, from rocks and caverns submarine,
With leathery branch, and bladdered buds between;
There, its dark folds the puckered laver spread,   195
With trees in miniature of various red;
There flag-shaped olive-leaves, depending hung,
And fairy fans from glossy pebbles sprung;
Then her terrestrial train the nereids meet,
And lay their spoils saline at Flora's feet.   200

Beachy Head

On thy stupendous summit, rock sublime!
That o'er the channel reared, halfway at sea
The mariner at early morning hails,
I would recline; while Fancy should go forth,
And represent the strange and awful hour   5
Of vast concussion; when the Omnipotent
Stretched forth his arm, and rent the solid hills,
Bidding the impetuous main flood rush between
The rifted shores, and from the continent
Eternally divided this green isle.   10
Imperial lord of the high southern coast!
From thy projecting headland I would mark
Far in the east the shades of night disperse,
Melting and thinned, as from the dark blue wave
Emerging, brilliant rays of arrowy light   15
Dart from the horizon; when the glorious sun
Just lifts above it his resplendent orb.
Advances now, with feathery silver touched,
The rippling tide of flood; glisten the sands,
While, inmates of the chalky clefts that scar   20
Thy sides precipitous, with shrill harsh cry,
Their white wings glancing in the level beam,
The terns, and gulls, and tarrocks, seek their food,
And thy rough hollows echo to the voice
Of the gray choughs, and ever restless daws,   25
With clamour, not unlike the chiding hounds,
While the lone shepherd, and his baying dog,
Drive to thy turfy crest his bleating flock.
The high meridian of the day is past,
And ocean now, reflecting the calm heaven,   30
Is of cerulean hue; and murmurs low
The tide of ebb, upon the level sands.
The sloop, her angular canvas shifting still,
Catches the light and variable airs
That but a little crisp the summer sea.   35
Dimpling its tranquil surface.

                    Afar off,
And just emerging from the arch immense

Where seem to part the elements, a fleet
Of fishing vessels stretch their lesser sails;
While more remote, and like a dubious spot   40
Just hanging in the horizon, laden deep,
The ship of commerce richly freighted, makes
Her slower progress, on her distant voyage,
Bound to the orient climates, where the sun
Matures the spice within its odorous shell,   45
And, rivalling the grey worm's filmy toil,
Bursts from its pod the vegetable down;
Which in long turbaned wreaths, from torrid heat
Defends the brows of Asia's countless castes.
There the earth hides within her glowing breast   50
The beamy adamant, and the round pearl
Encased in rugged covering; which the slave,
With perilous and breathless toil, tears off
From the rough sea-rock, deep beneath the waves.
These are the toys of nature; and her sport   55
Of little estimate in reason's eye:
And they who reason, with abhorrence see
Man, for such gaudes and baubles, violate
The sacred freedom of his fellow man –
Erroneous estimate! As heaven's pure air,   60
Fresh as it blows on this aërial height,
Or sound of seas upon the stony strand,
Or inland, the gay harmony of birds,
And winds that wander in the leafy woods;
Are to the unadulterate taste more worth   65
Than the elaborate harmony, brought out
From fretted stop, or modulated airs
Of vocal science. So the brightest gems,
Glancing resplendent on the regal crown,
Or trembling in the high born beauty's ear,   70
Are poor and paltry, to the lovely light
Of the fair star, that as the day declines,
Attendant on her queen, the crescent moon,
Bathes her bright tresses in the eastern wave.
For now the sun is verging to the sea,   75
And as he westward sinks, the floating clouds
Suspended, move upon the evening gale,
And gathering round his orb, as if to shade

41

The insufferable brightness, they resign
Their gauzy whiteness; and more warmed, assume   80
All hues of purple. There, transparent gold
Mingles with ruby tints, and sapphire gleams,
And colours, such as nature through her world
Shows only in the ethereal canopy.
Thither aspiring Fancy fondly soars,   85
Wandering sublime thro' visionary vales,
Where bright pavilions rise, and trophies, fanned
By airs celestial; and adorned with wreaths
Of flowers that bloom amid elysian bowers.
Now bright, and brighter still the colours glow,   90
Till half the lustrous orb within the flood
Seems to retire: the flood reflecting still
Its splendour, and in mimic glory dressed;
Till the last ray shot upward, fires the clouds
With blazing crimson; then in paler light,   95
Long lines of tenderer radiance, lingering yield
To partial darkness; and on the opposing side
The early moon distinctly rising, throws
Her pearly brilliance on the trembling tide.
The fishermen, who at set seasons pass   100
Many a league off at sea their toiling night,
Now hail their comrades, from their daily task
Returning; and make ready for their own,
With the night tide commencing. The night tide
Bears a dark vessel on, whose hull and sails   105
Mark her a coaster from the north. Her keel
Now ploughs the sand; and sidelong now she leans,
While with loud clamours her athletic crew
Unload her; and resounds the busy hum
Along the wave-worn rocks. Yet more remote,   110
Where the rough cliff hangs beetling o'er its base,
All breathes repose; the water's rippling sound
Scarce heard; but now and then the sea-snipe's cry
Just tells that something living is abroad;
And sometimes crossing on the moon-bright line,   115
Glimmers the skiff, faintly discerned awhile,
Then lost in shadow.

Contemplation here,
High on her throne of rock, aloof may sit,
And bid recording Memory unfold
Her scroll voluminous – bid her retrace   120
The period, when from Neustria's hostile shore
The Norman launched his galleys, and the bay
O'er which that mass of ruin frowns even now
In vain and sullen menace, then received
The new invaders; a proud martial race,   125
Of Scandinavia the undaunted sons,
Whom Dogon, Fier-a-bras, and Humfroi led
To conquest: while Trinacria to their power
Yielded her wheaten garland; and when thou,
Parthenope! within thy fertile bay   130
Received the victors.

        In the mailed ranks
Of Normans landing on the British coast
Rode Taillefer; and with astounding voice
Thundered the war song daring Roland sang
First in the fierce contention: vainly brave,   135
One not inglorious struggle England made –
But failing, saw the Saxon heptarchy
Finish for ever. Then the holy pile,
Yet seen upon the field of conquest, rose,
Where to appease heaven's wrath for so much blood,   140
The conqueror bade unceasing prayers ascend,
And requiems for the slayers and the slain.
But let not modern Gallia form from hence
Presumptuous hopes, that ever thou again,
Queen of the isles! shalt crouch to foreign arms.   145
The enervate sons of Italy may yield;
And the Iberian, all his trophies torn
And wrapped in Superstition's monkish weed,
May shelter his abasement, and put on
Degrading fetters. Never, never thou!   150
Imperial mistress of the obedient sea;
But thou, in thy integrity secure,
Shalt now undaunted meet a world in arms.

England! 'Twas where this promontory rears
Its rugged brow above the channel wave,   155
Parting the hostile nations, that thy fame,
Thy naval fame was tarnished, at what time
Thou, leagued with the Batavian, gavest to France
One day of triumph – triumph the more loud,
Because even then so rare. Oh! well redeemed,   160
Since, by a series of illustrious men,
Such as no other country ever reared,
To vindicate her cause. It is a list
Which, as Fame echoes it, blanches the cheek
Of bold Ambition; while the despot feels   165
The extorted sceptre tremble in his grasp.
From even the proudest roll by glory filled,
How gladly the reflecting mind returns
To simple scenes of peace and industry,
Where, bosomed in some valley of the hills   170
Stands the lone farm; its gate with tawny ricks
Surrounded, and with granaries and sheds,
Roofed with green mosses, and by elms and ash
Partially shaded; and not far removed
The hut of sea-flints built; the humble home   175
Of one, who sometimes watches on the heights,
When hid in the cold mist of passing clouds,
The flock, with dripping fleeces, are dispersed
O'er the wide down; then from some ridged point
That overlooks the sea, his eager eye   180
Watches the bark that for his signal waits
To land its merchandise – quitting for this
Clandestine traffic his more honest toil,
The crook abandoning, he braves himself
The heaviest snowstorm of December's night,   185
When with conflicting winds the ocean raves,
And on the tossing boat, unfearing mounts
To meet the partners of the perilous trade,
And share their hazard. Well it were for him,
If no such commerce of destruction known,   190
He were content with what the earth affords
To human labour; even where she seems
Reluctant most. More happy is the hind,
Who, with his own hands rears on some black moor,

44

Or turbary, his independent hut   195
Covered with heather, whence the slow white smoke
Of smouldering peat arises. A few sheep,
His best possession, with his children share
The rugged shed when wintry tempests blow;
But, when with spring's return the green blades rise   200
Amid the russet heath, the household live
Joint tenants of the waste throughout the day,
And often, from her nest, among the swamps,
Where the gemmed sundew grows, or fringed buckbean,
They scare the plover, that with plaintive cries   205
Flutters, as sorely wounded, down the wind.
Rude, and but just removed from savage life
Is the rough dweller among scenes like these,
'Scenes all unlike the poet's fabling dreams
Describing Arcady'. But he is free;   210
The dread that follows on illegal acts
He never feels; and his industrious mate
Shares in his labour. Where the brook is traced
By crowding osiers, and the black coot hides
Among the plashy reeds, her diving brood,   215
The matron wades; gathering the long green rush
That well prepared hereafter lends its light
To her poor cottage, dark and cheerless else
Thro' the drear hours of winter. Otherwhile
She leads her infant group where charlock grows   220
'Unprofitably gay', or to the fields,
Where congregate the linnet and the finch,
That on the thistles, so profusely spread,
Feast in the desert; the poor family
Early resort, extirpating with care   225
These, and the gaudier mischief of the ground;
Then flames the high raised heap; seen afar off
Like hostile war-fires flashing to the sky.
Another task is theirs: on fields that show
As angry heaven had rained sterility,   230
Stony and cold, and hostile to the plough,
Where clamouring loud, the evening curlew runs
And drops her spotted eggs among the flints;
The mother and the children pile the stones
In rugged pyramids; and all this toil   235

They patiently encounter; well content
On their flock bed to slumber undisturbed
Beneath the smoky roof they call their own.
Oh! little knows the sturdy hind, who stands
Gazing, with looks where envy and contempt   240
Are often strangely mingled, on the car
Where prosperous Fortune sits; what secret care
Or sick satiety is often hid,
Beneath the splendid outside. He knows not
How frequently the child of luxury   245
Enjoying nothing, flies from place to place
In chase of pleasure that eludes his grasp;
And that content is e'en less found by him,
Than by the labourer, whose pickaxe smoothes
The road before his chariot; and who doffs   250
What was a hat; and as the train pass on,
Thinks how one day's expenditure, like this,
Would cheer him for long months, when to his toil
The frozen earth closes her marble breast.
Ah! who *is* happy? Happiness! A word   255
That like false fire, from marsh effluvia born,
Misleads the wanderer, destined to contend
In the world's wilderness, with want or woe –
Yet *they* are happy, who have never asked
What good or evil means. The boy   260
That on the river's margin gaily plays,
Has heard that death is there – he knows not death,
And therefore fears it not; and venturing in
He gains a bullrush, or a minnow – then,
At certain peril, for a worthless prize,   265
A crow's, or raven's nest, he climbs the bole,
Of some tall pine; and of his prowess proud,
Is for a moment happy. Are *your* cares,
Ye who despise him, never worse applied?
The village girl is happy, who sets forth   270
To distant fair, gay in her Sunday suit,
With cherry-coloured knots, and flourished shawl,
And bonnet newly purchased. So is he
Her little brother, who his mimic drum
Beats, till he drowns her rural lovers' oaths   275
Of constant faith and still-increasing love;

46

Ah! yet a while, and half those oaths believed,
Her happiness is vanished; and the boy
While yet a stripling, finds the sound he loved
Has led him on, till he has given up   280
His freedom, and his happiness together.
I *once* was happy, when while yet a child,
I learned to love these upland solitudes,
And, when elastic as the mountain air,
To my light spirit, care was yet unknown   285
And evil unforeseen. Early it came,
And childhood scarcely passed, I was condemned,
A guiltless exile, silently to sigh,
While Memory, with faithful pencil, drew
The contrast; and regretting, I compared   290
With the polluted smoky atmosphere
And dark and stifling streets, the southern hills
That to the setting sun, their graceful heads
Rearing, o'erlook the frith, where Vecta breaks
With her white rocks, the strong impetuous tide,   295
When western winds the vast Atlantic urge
To thunder on the coast. Haunts of my youth!
Scenes of fond daydreams, I behold ye yet!
Where 'twas so pleasant by thy northern slopes
To climb the winding sheep-path, aided oft   300
By scattered thorns, whose spiny branches bore
Small woolly tufts, spoils of the vagrant lamb
There seeking shelter from the noonday sun;
And pleasant, seated on the short soft turf,
To look beneath upon the hollow way   305
While heavily upward moved the labouring wain,
And stalking slowly by, the sturdy hind
To ease his panting team, stopped with a stone
The grating wheel.

            Advancing higher still
The prospect widens, and the village church   310
But little, o'er the lowly roofs around
Rears its grey belfry, and its simple vane;
Those lowly roofs of thatch are half concealed
By the rude arms of trees, lovely in spring,
When on each bough, the rosy-tinctured bloom   315

Sits thick, and promises autumnal plenty.
For even those orchards round the Norman farms,
Which, as their owners mark the promised fruit,
Console them for the vineyards of the south,
Surpass not these.

              Where woods of ash, and beech,   320
And partial copses, fringe the green hill-foot,
The upland shepherd rears his modest home,
There wanders by, a little nameless stream
That from the hill wells forth, bright now and clear,
Or after rain with chalky mixture grey,   325
But still refreshing in its shallow course,
The cottage garden; most for use designed,
Yet not of beauty destitute. The vine
Mantles the little casement; yet the briar
Drops fragrant dew among the July flowers;   330
And pansies rayed, and freaked and mottled pinks
Grow among balm, and rosemary and rue.
There honeysuckles flaunt, and roses blow
Almost uncultured: some with dark green leaves
Contrast their flowers of pure unsullied white;   335
Others, like velvet robes of regal state
Of richest crimson, while in thorny moss
Enshrined and cradled, the most lovely, wear
The hues of youthful beauty's glowing cheek.
With fond regret I recollect e'en now   340
In spring and summer, what delight I felt
Among these cottage gardens, and how much
Such artless nosegays, knotted with a rush
By village housewife or her ruddy maid,
Were welcome to me; soon and simply pleased.   345

An early worshipper at nature's shrine;
I loved her rudest scenes – warrens, and heaths,
And yellow commons, and birch-shaded hollows,
And hedgerows, bordering unfrequented lanes
Bowered with wild roses, and the clasping woodbine   350
Where purple tassels of the tangling vetch
With bittersweet, and bryony inweave,
And the dew fills the silver bindweed's cups –

I loved to trace the brooks whose humid banks
Nourish the harebell, and the freckled pagil;   355
And stroll among o'ershadowing woods of beech,
Lending in summer, from the heats of noon
A whispering shade; while haply there reclines
Some pensive lover of uncultured flowers,
Who, from the tumps with bright green mosses clad,   360
Plucks the wood sorrel, with its light thin leaves,
Heart-shaped, and triply folded; and its root
Creeping like beaded coral; or who there
Gathers, the copse's pride, anemones,
With rays like golden studs on ivory laid   365
Most delicate: but touched with purple clouds,
Fit crown for April's fair but changeful brow.

Ah! hills so early loved! in fancy still
I breathe your pure keen air; and still behold
Those widely spreading views, mocking alike   370
The poet and the painter's utmost art.
And still, observing objects more minute,
Wondering remark the strange and foreign forms
Of seashells; with the pale calcareous soil
Mingled, and seeming of resembling substance.   375
Tho' surely the blue ocean 'from the heights
Where the Downs westward trend, but dimly seen'
Here never rolled its surge. Does nature then
Mimic, in wanton mood, fantastic shapes
Of bivalves, and inwreathed volutes, that cling   380
To the dark sea-rock of the wat'ry world?
Or did this range of chalky mountains, once
Form a vast basin, where the ocean waves
Swelled fathomless? What time these fossil shells,
Buoyed on their native element, were thrown   385
Among the imbedding calx: when the huge hill
Its giant bulk heaved, and in strange ferment
Grew up a guardian barrier, 'twixt the sea
And the green level of the sylvan weald.

Ah! very vain is science' proudest boast,   390
And but a little light its flame yet lends
To its most ardent votaries; since from whence

49

These fossil forms are seen, is but conjecture,
Food for vague theories, or vain dispute,
While to his daily task the peasant goes,   395
Unheeding such inquiry; with no care
But that the kindly change of sun and shower,
Fit for his toil the earth he cultivates.
As little recks the herdsman of the hill,
Who on some turfy knoll, idly reclined,   400
Watches his wether flock; that deep beneath
Rest the remains of men, of whom is left
No traces in the records of mankind,
Save what these half obliterated mounds
And half filled trenches doubtfully impart   405
To some lone antiquary; who on times remote,
Since which two thousand years have rolled away,
Loves to contemplate. He perhaps may trace,
Or fancy he can trace, the oblong square
Where the mailed legions, under Claudius, reared,   410
The rampire, or excavated fossé delved;
What time the huge unwieldy elephant
Auxiliary reluctant, hither led,
From Afric's forest glooms and tawny sands,
First felt the northern blast, and his vast frame   415
Sunk useless; whence in after ages found,
The wondering hinds, on those enormous bones
Gazed; and in giants dwelling on the hills
Believed and marvelled.

                        Hither, Ambition, come!
Come and behold the nothingness of all   420
For which you carry thro' the oppressed earth,
War, and its train of horrors – see where tread
The innumerous hoofs of flocks above the works
By which the warrior sought to register
His glory, and immortalise his name –   425
The pirate Dane, who from his circular camp
Bore in destructive robbery, fire and sword
Down thro' the vale, sleeps unremembered here;
And here, beneath the green sward, rests alike
The savage native, who his acorn meal   430
Shared with the herds, that ranged the pathless woods;

And the centurion, who on these wide hills
Encamping, planted the imperial eagle.
All, with the lapse of time, have passed away,
Even as the clouds, with dark and dragon shapes,   435
Or like vast promontories crowned with towers,
Cast their broad shadows on the downs: then sail
Far to the northward, and their transient gloom
Is soon forgotten.

               But from thoughts like these,
By human crimes suggested, let us turn   440
To where a more attractive study courts
The wanderer of the hills; while shepherd girls
Will from among the fescue bring him flowers,
Of wonderous mockery; some resembling bees
In velvet vest, intent on their sweet toil,   445
While others mimic flies, that lightly sport
In the green shade, or float along the pool,
But here seem perched upon the slender stalk,
And gathering honeydew. While in the breeze
That wafts the thistle's plumed seed along,   450
Bluebells wave tremulous. The mountain thyme
Purples the hassock of the heaving mole,
And the short turf is gay with tormentil,
And bird's foot trefoil, and the lesser tribes
Of hawkweed; spangling it with fringed stars.   455
Near where a richer tract of cultured land
Slopes to the south; and burnished by the sun,
Bend in the gale of August, floods of corn;
The guardian of the flock, with watchful care,
Repels by voice and dog the encroaching sheep –   460
While his boy visits every wired trap
That scars the turf; and from the pit-falls takes
The timid migrants, who from distant wilds,
Warrens, and stone quarries, are destined thus
To lose their short existence. But unsought   465
By luxury yet, the shepherd still protects
The social bird, who from his native haunts
Of willowy current, or the rushy pool,
Follows the fleecy crowd, and flirts and skims,
In fellowship among them.

More elevated takes the changeful winds,
The windmill rears its vanes; and thitherward
With his white load, the master travelling,
Scarce the rooks rising slow on whispering wings,
While o'er his head, before the summer sun   475
Lights up the blue expanse, heard more than seen,
The lark sings matins; and above the clouds
Floating, embathes his spotted breast in dew.
Beneath the shadow of a gnarled thorn,
Bent by the sea blast, from a seat of turf   480
With fairy nosegays strewn, how wide the view!
Till in the distant north it melts away,
And mingles indiscriminate with clouds:
But if the eye could reach so far, the mart
Of England's capital, its domes and spires   485
Might be perceived. Yet hence the distant range
Of Kentish hills, appear in purple haze;
And nearer, undulate the wooded heights,
And airy summits, that above the mole
Rise in green beauty; and the beaconed ridge   490
Of Black Down shagged with heath, and swelling rude
Like a dark island from the vale; its brow
Catching the last rays of the evening sun
That gleam between the nearer park's old oaks,
Then lighten up the river, and make prominent   495
The portal, and the ruined battlements
Of that dismantled fortress; raised what time
The Conqueror's successors fiercely fought,
Tearing with civil feuds the desolate land.
But now a tiller of the soil dwells there,   500
And of the turret's looped and raftered halls
Has made a humbler homestead – where he sees,
Instead of armed foemen, herds that graze
Along his yellow meadows; or his flocks
At evening from the upland driv'n to fold.   505

In such a castellated mansion once
A stranger chose his home; and where hard by
In rude disorder fallen, and hid with brushwood
Lay fragments grey of towers and buttresses,

Among the ruins, often he would muse –   510
His rustic meal soon ended, he was wont
To wander forth, listening the evening sounds
Of rushing mill dam, or the distant team,
Or nightjar, chasing fern-flies: the tired hind
Passed him at nightfall, wondering he should sit   515
On the hill top so late: they from the coast
Who sought bye paths with their clandestine load,
Saw with suspicious doubt, the lonely man
Cross on their way: but village maidens thought
His senses injured; and with pity say   520
That he, poor youth! must have been crossed in love –
For often, stretched upon the mountain turf
With folded arms, and eyes intently fixed
Where ancient elms and firs obscured a grange,
Some little space within the vale below,   525
They heard him, as complaining of his fate,
And to the murmuring wind, of cold neglect
And baffled hope he told. The peasant girls
These plaintive sounds remember, and even now
Among them may be heard the stranger's songs.   530

Were I a shepherd on the hill
        And ever as the mists withdrew
Could see the willows of the rill
Shading the footway to the mill
        Where once I walked with you –   535

And as away night's shadows sail,
        And sounds of birds and brooks arise,
Believe, that from the woody vale
I hear your voice upon the gale
        In soothing melodies;   540

And viewing from the Alpine height,
        The prospect dressed in hues of air,
Could say, while transient colours bright
Touched the fair scene with dewy light,
        'Tis, that *her* eyes are there!   545

I think, I could endure my lot
        And linger on a few short years,
And then, by all but you forgot,
Sleep, where the turf that clothes the spot
        May claim some pitying tears.   550

For 'tis not easy to forget
        One, who thro' life has loved you still,
And you, however late, might yet
With sighs to memory giv'n, regret
        The Shepherd of the Hill.   555

Yet otherwhile it seemed as if young Hope
Her flattering pencil gave to Fancy's hand,
And in his wanderings, reared to sooth his soul
Ideal bowers of pleasure. Then, of solitude
And of his hermit life, still more enamoured,   560
His home was in the forest; and wild fruits
And bread sustained him. There in early spring
The barkmen found him, e'er the sun arose;
There at their daily toil, the wedgecutters
Beheld him thro' the distant thicket move.   565
The shaggy dog following the truffle hunter,
Barked at the loiterer; and perchance at night
Belated villagers from fair or wake,
While the fresh night-wind let the moonbeams in
Between the swaying boughs, just saw him pass,   570
And then in silence, gliding like a ghost
He vanished! lost among the deepening gloom.
But near one ancient tree, whose wreathed roots
Formed a rude couch, love-songs and scattered rhymes,
Unfinished sentences, or half erased,   575
And rhapsodies like this, were sometimes found –

Let us to woodland wilds repair
        While yet the glittering night-dews seem
To wait the freshly-breathing air,
        Precursive of the morning beam,   580
That rising with advancing day,
Scatters the silver drops away.

An elm, uprooted by the storm,
　　The trunk with mosses grey and green,
Shall make for us a rustic form,　　　　　　　　　585
　　Where lighter grows the forest scene;
And far among the bowery shades,
Are ferny lawns and grassy glades.

Retiring May to lovely June
　　Her latest garland now resigns;　　　　　　　590
The banks with cuckoo-flowers are strewn,
　　The wood-walks blue with columbines,
And with its reeds, the wandering stream
Reflects the flag-flower's golden gleam.

There, feathering down the turf to meet,　　　　　595
　　Their shadowy arms the beeches spread,
While high above our sylvan seat,
　　Lifts the light ash its airy head;
And later leaved, the oaks between
Extend their bows of vernal green.　　　　　　　600

The slender birch its paper rind
　　Seems offering to divided love,
And shuddering even without a wind
　　Aspens, their paler foliage move,
As if some spirit of the air　　　　　　　　　　605
Breathed a low sigh in passing there.

The squirrel in his frolic mood,
　　Will fearless bound among the boughs;
Yaffils laugh loudly thro' the wood,
　　And murmuring ring-doves tell their vows;　　610
While we, as sweetest wood-scents rise,
Listen to woodland melodies.

And I'll contrive a sylvan room
　　Against the time of summer heat,
Where leaves, inwoven in nature's loom,　　　　615
　　Shall canopy our green retreat;
And gales that 'close the eye of day'
Shall linger, e'er they die away.

And when a sear and sallow hue
    From early frost the bower receives,   620
I'll dress the sand rock cave for you,
    And strew the floor with heath and leaves,
That you, against the autumnal air
May find securer shelter there.

The nightingale will then have ceased   625
    To sing her moonlight serenade;
But the gay bird with blushing breast,
    And woodlarks still will haunt the shade,
And by the borders of the spring
Reed-wrens will yet be carolling.   630

The forest hermit's lonely cave
    None but such soothing sounds shall reach,
Or hardly heard, the distant wave
    Slow breaking on the stony beach;
Or winds, that now sigh soft and low,   635
Now make wild music as they blow.

And then, before the chilling north
    The tawny foliage falling light
Seems, as it flits along the earth,
    The footfall of the busy sprite,   640
Who wrapt in pale autumnal gloom,
Calls up the mist-born mushroom.

Oh! could I hear your soft voice there,
    And see you in the forest green
All beauteous as you are, more fair   645
    You'd look, amid the sylvan scene,
And in a wood-girl's simple guise,
Be still more lovely in mine eyes.

Ye phantoms of unreal delight,
    Visions of fond delirium born!   650
Rise not on my deluded sight,
    Then leave me drooping and forlorn
To know, such bliss can never be,
Unless —— loved like me.

The visionary, nursing dreams like these,   655
Is not indeed unhappy. Summer woods
Wave over him, and whisper as they wave,
Some future blessings he may yet enjoy.
And as above him sail the silver clouds,
He follows them in thought to distant climes,   660
Where, far from the cold policy of this,
Dividing him from her he fondly loves,
He, in some island of the southern sea,
May haply build his cane-constructed bower
Beneath the breadfruit, or aspiring palm,   665
With long green foliage rippling in the gale.
Oh! let him cherish his ideal bliss –
For what is life, when Hope has ceased to strew
Her fragile flowers along its thorny way?
And sad and gloomy are his days, who lives   670
Of Hope abandoned!

              Just beneath the rock
Where Beachy overpeers the channel wave,
Within a cavern mined by wintry tides
Dwelt one, who long disgusted with the world
And all its ways, appeared to suffer life   675
Rather than live; the soul-reviving gale,
Fanning the beanfield, or the thymy heath,
Had not for many summers breathed on him;
And nothing marked to him the season's change,
Save that more gently rose the placid sea,   680
And that the birds which winter on the coast
Gave place to other migrants; save that the fog,
Hovering no more above the beetling cliffs
Betrayed not then the little careless sheep
On the brink grazing, while their headlong fall   685
Near the lone hermit's flint-surrounded home,
Claimed unavailing pity; for his heart
Was feelingly alive to all that breathed;
And outraged as he was, in sanguine youth,
By human crimes, he still acutely felt   690
For human misery.

              Wandering on the beach,
He learned to augur from the clouds of heaven,

And from the changing colours of the sea,
And sullen murmurs of the hollow cliffs,
Or the dark porpoises, that near the shore   695
Gambolled and sported on the level brine
When tempests were approaching: then at night
He listened to the wind; and as it drove
The billows with o'erwhelming vehemence
He, starting from his rugged couch, went forth   700
And hazarding a life, too valueless,
He waded thro' the waves, with plank or pole
Towards where the mariner in conflict dread
Was buffeting for life the roaring surge;
And now just seen, now lost in foaming gulfs,   705
The dismal gleaming of the clouded moon
Showed the dire peril. Often he had snatched
From the wild billows, some unhappy man
Who lived to bless the hermit of the rocks.
But if his generous cares were all in vain,   710
And with slow swell the tide of morning bore
Some blue swol'n corse to land; the pale recluse
Dug in the chalk a sepulchre – above
Where the dank sea-wrack marked the utmost tide,
And with his prayers performed the obsequies   715
For the poor helpless stranger.

                         One dark night
The equinoctial wind blew south by west,
Fierce on the shore – the bellowing cliffs were shook
Even to their stony base, and fragments fell
Flashing and thundering on the angry flood.   720
At daybreak, anxious for the lonely man,
His cave the mountain shepherds visited,
Tho' sand and banks of weeds had choked their way.
He was not in it; but his drowned corse
By the waves wafted, near his former home   725
Received the rites of burial. Those who read
Chiselled within the rock, these mournful lines,
Memorials of his sufferings, did not grieve,
That dying in the cause of charity
His spirit, from its earthly bondage freed,   730
Had to some better region fled for ever.

NOTES

Sonnet V
Aruna: the river Arun in Sussex, close to Smith's childhood home at
Bignor Park.

Sonnet XXII
Smith wrote five sonnets in the person of Werther. Goethe's immensely
influential epistolary novel *The Sorrows of Young Werther* (1774) recounts
the sufferings and eventual suicide of a sensitive artist at odds with society
and unhappy in love.

Sonnet XXVI
Fanes: an archaic word for temples.
Thomas Otway (1652–85): Smith's note to the sonnet records that Otway's
father was rector of Woolbeding, a village on the banks of the Arun, where
Smith also lived for a time after leaving her husband. Otway died in
poverty.

Sonnet XXXI
This sonnet dates from Smith's return to Sussex after her stay in the King's
Bench prison with her husband.

Sonnet XL
The sonnet originally appeared in Smith's novel *Emmeline* (1788), where
it is written by the heroine.

Sonnets XLIX and LI
These sonnets originally appeared in Smith's novel *Celestina* (1791), where
they are written by the heroine.

Sonnet LXVI
Smith's note records that this sonnet was written during a storm in 1791.
She later published it in her novel *Montalbert* (1795) before including it in
the *Elegiac Sonnets*.

Sonnet LXVII
This sonnet, like LXVI, was first published in *Montalbert* (1795).

Sonnet LXXVII
Smith included a long note on natural history, quoting from the
Encyclopaedia Britannica, Erasmus Darwin and Shakespeare on the
phenomenon of the floating threads of small spiders. The sonnet was
included in her *Conversations Introducing Poetry* (1804), where she added

a note on Gilbert White's observation of a shower of such gossamer spiders' webs that fell on the village of Selbourne on 21 September 1741.

Sonnet LXXVIII
The sonnet, like XCI, probably alludes to the death of Smith's daughter Augusta in 1795, at the age of twenty.

Sonnet LXXIX
Smith's note to this sonnet quotes from Rousseau's *Rêveries du promeneur solitaire* (1782), comparing his account of turning to the study of botany for solace with her own recourse to it as an escape from the problems that beset her.

Sonnets LXXXVI and LXXXVII
These sonnets were first published in Smith's novel *The Young Philosopher* (1798).

Thirty-Eight
The poem is addressed to Eliza Hayley, the wife of Smith's patron, the poet William Hayley, to whom *Elegiac Sonnets* was dedicated.

Verses Supposed to have been Written in the New Forest, in Early Spring
The poem was first published in Smith's novel *Marchmont* (1796), where it is written by the title character. It is accompanied in *Elegiac Sonnets* by Smith's note on the growth habits of mosses and lichens, and on the different species and habitats of the flowers in the poem. Pilewort, annotated by Smith as Ranuncula ficaria, is the Lesser Celandine, Ranunculus ficaria. Jacinths she annotates as Hyacinthus non scriptus or harebell. Windflower is another name for the wood anemone.

The Forest Boy
Smith's note to this poem acknowledges the influence of Robert Southey's poem 'Mary, the Maid of the Inn' (1797), and also links it to her own experience of war: 'I, who have been so sad a sufferer in this miserable contest my well endeavour to associate myself with those who apply what powers they have to deprecate the horrors of war.' One of her sons had been seriously wounded in the Siege of Dunkirk in 1793.
hurst: a wooded hill.

The Emigrants
Book the First
Brighthelmstone: the original name for Brighton, where Smith lived for a time.
The scene is set immediately following the autumn massacres and the declaration of the republic in France.

Book the Second
The scene is set a few months after the execution of Louis XVI and the outbreak of war between England and France.

The second book of *The Emigrants* is introduced by an epigraph from Virgil, *Georgics* I. 505–11, which reads in part, 'Right has become wrong and wrong has become right: war has spread through the world. The plough is neglected, the fields are empty, the sickle has been beaten into the sword.'

The Hedgehog Seen in a Frequented Path
Stuart Curran notes in *The Poems of Charlotte Smith* that 'negro' here denotes the black colour of the hedgehog's face.
l. 24 *noli me tangere*: 'do not touch me'.

To the Firefly of Jamaica, Seen in a Collection
Smith's father-in-law was an East India Company merchant with slave trade connections. He had lived in Barbados, where his first wife had been brought up, and where the family owned estates and slaves.
Smith's notes to the poem give the botanical names of the tropical flora referred to. 'Guazame' is Theobroma guazama, the Great Cedar of Jamaica, 'swietan' is mahogany. Plumeria she annotates as 'Tree Jasmin'. 'Granate' is the pomegranate, 'Plinia' Smith annotates as Plinia pedunculata, 'a fragrant native of tropical countires'. The common name is the Surinam Cherry. The shaddock, she notes, 'is shaped like a lemon with the colour of an orange; it is sometimes as big as the largest melon; but not very good to eat. At least those I have formerly seen brought from Barbados were worth nothing.' The fruit is the ancestor of the grapefruit.

To a Geranium which Flowered during the Winter. Written in Autumn
Smith's note to the poem records the account, given to her by a friend who had visited the Cape of Good Hope, of the plants growing luxuriantly in the wild. 'Caffres' (l. 4) is annotated by her as the term for the peoples who live around the Cape.

Flora
The poem is included in *Beachy Head and Other Poems* (1807). Smith annotates the scientific terms, with the exception of Cypripedium (l. 36), which is (appropriately) the Lady's Slipper orchid. Scandix (l. 45) she terms 'Venus's comb, or Shepherd's needle'; 'Anthoxanthum' (l. 48), 'vernal meadow grass' (Anthoxanthum odoratum).
'Polyp' (l. 182) Smith annotates as the sea anemone; 'corraline' (l. 184) 'is, if I do not misunderstand the only book I have to consult, a shelly substance, the work of sea insects, adhering to stones and seaweeds'; 'green byssus' (l. 189) she explains as 'a semi-transparent substance floating on the waves'. It is made of the threads by which the species of molluscs known as Pinna (l. 192) attach themselves to rocks.

Beachy Head
l. 23 tarrocks: Smith annotates this as Larus tridactylus. The common modern name is the kittiwake.
l. 47 'the vegetable down' is annotated by Smith as 'cotton'.
l. 121 Neustria: Normandy.

l. 127 Dogon, Fier-a-bras, Humfroi: Smith's long note explains the historical background. The three were Normans, brothers who ruled Sicily in the tenth century.

l. 128 Trinacria: Smith annotates as the ancient name for Sicily.

l. 197 Saxon heptarchy: the seven kingdoms of England in Saxon times.

l. 133 Taillefer: Smith's note recounts how he led the Normans to the battle against the English king Harold, singing a war song, and was killed in the first charge.

l. 143 Gallia: France.

l. 158 the Batavian: Smith annotates the historical background. In 1690 a combined English and Dutch fleet fought and were defeated by the French, with great losses.

l. 193 hind: farmworker, peasant.

l. 195 turbary: land from which peat may be cut for fuel.

l. 228 like hostile war-fires': Smith annotates this as the beacons formerly used to warn of the approach of an enemy.

l. 237 flock bed: a mattress filled with wool.

l. 294 frith: firth, inlet. Vecta is the Isle of Wight.

l. ll. 347–8 warrens, heaths, commons: 'warrens' were pieces of land enclosed for breeding game, and hence left wild, 'heath' is moorland, 'commons' is the term for common land, which would have been unenclosed and uncultivated.

l. 352 bittersweet: Smith annotates as Solanum dulcamara. Usually known now as Woody Nightshade.

l. 355 pagil: annotated by Smith as Primula veris, which is the cowslip. She gives no alternative common name, suggesting that she considered this the usual English name. Usually spelled paigle, it is now a dialect name for cowslips in southern England (Geoffrey Grigson, *The Englishman's Flora*, London, Phoenix House 1958).

l. 360 tumps: a dialect term for mounds or hillocks.

ll. 382–3 Smith's note acknowledges that she took the idea that the Downs had once been covered by sea, hence the presence of sea shells in the chalk, from 'an idea started by Mr White' (Gilbert White). She records finding shells among the chalk 'some quite in a fossil state', 'which excited my surprise'; 'nor was I ever satisfied with the attempts to explain many of the phenomena which call forth conjecture in those books I happened to have had access to on this subject'.

l. 386 calx: limestone.

l. 401 wether flock: a wether is a castrated male sheep. The term refers to sheep kept for wool, as opposed to a breeding flock.

ll. 412–19 Smith writes at length about the excavation of elephant bones in Sussex in 1740, and theories of their possible origins.

ll. 443–6 fescue: a type of grass found on the Downs. The lines following refer to Bee Orchids and Fly Orchids, downland plants whose flowers mimic the appearance of bees and flys.

l. 459 Smith's note records that, particularly on the southern Downs, shepherds have to be particularly vigilant to prevent sheep from encroaching onto cultivated land.

l. 461 'wired trap' Smith annotates as traps in the turf to catch wheatears

– and takes issue with Gilbert White regarding the birds' habitat.

l. 467 social bird: Smith annotates as the yellow wagtail, which frequents flocks to feed on insects.

l. 491 Black Down: Smith annotates as a high ridge between Sussex and Surrey.

ll. 563–4 barkmen, wedgecutters: Smith annotates the first as the term for the men who mark trees to be felled by cutting their bark, and 'wedgecutters' as those who cut the beechwood wedges used in shipbuilding, an important part of the economy of the Downs.

l. 594 flag-flower: annotated by Smith as Iris pseudacorus. The yellow flag iris.

l. 609 yaffils: a dialect word for the green woodpecker.

l. 663 'island in the southern sea' refers to the European discovery of Tahiti. Smith's note reads: 'An allusion to the visionary delights of the newly discovered island where it was first believed men lived in a state of simplicity and happiness, but where, as later enquiries ascertained, that exemption from toil, which the fertility of their country gives them, produces the greatest vices; and a degree of corruption that late navigators think will end in the extirpation of the whole people in a few years.'

l. 674 Smith's note recounts the legend, which she had heard thirty years earlier, of the recluse who lived in a cave under Beachy Head.

Fyfield*Books*

Two millennia of essential classics

The extensive FyfieldBooks list includes

Djuna Barnes *The Book of Repulsive Women and other poems*
edited by Rebecca Loncraine

Elizabeth Barrett Browning *Selected Poems* edited by Malcolm Hicks

Charles Baudelaire *Complete Poems in French and English*
translated by Walter Martin

Thomas Lovell Beddoes *Death's Jest-Book* edited by Michael Bradshaw

Aphra Behn *Selected Poems*
edited by Malcolm Hicks

Border Ballads: A Selection
edited by James Reed

The Brontë Sisters *Selected Poems*
edited by Stevie Davies

Sir Thomas Browne *Selected Writings*
edited by Claire Preston

Lewis Carroll *Selected Poems*
edited by Keith Silver

Paul Celan *Collected Prose*
translated by Rosmarie Waldrop

Thomas Chatterton *Selected Poems*
edited by Grevel Lindop

John Clare *By Himself*
edited by Eric Robinson and David Powell

Arthur Hugh Clough *Selected Poems*
edited by Shirley Chew

Samuel Taylor Coleridge *Selected Poetry* edited by William Empson and David Pirie

Tristan Corbière *The Centenary Corbière*
in French and English
translated by Val Warner

William Cowper *Selected Poems*
edited by Nick Rhodes

Gabriele d'Annunzio *Halcyon*
translated by J.G. Nichols

John Donne *Selected Letters*
edited by P.M. Oliver

William Dunbar *Selected Poems*
edited by Harriet Harvey Wood

Anne Finch, Countess of Winchilsea
Selected Poems
edited by Denys Thompson

Ford Madox Ford *Selected Poems*
edited by Max Saunders

John Gay *Selected Poems*
edited by Marcus Walsh

Oliver Goldsmith *Selected Writings*
edited by John Lucas

Robert Herrick *Selected Poems*
edited by David Jesson-Dibley

Victor Hugo *Selected Poetry*
in French and English
translated by Steven Monte

T.E. Hulme *Selected Writings*
edited by Patrick McGuinness

Leigh Hunt *Selected Writings*
edited by David Jesson Dibley

Wyndham Lewis *Collected Poems and Plays* edited by Alan Munton

Charles Lamb *Selected Writings*
edited by J.E. Morpurgo

Lucretius *De Rerum Natura: The Poem on Nature*
translated by C.H. Sisson

John Lyly *Selected Prose and Dramatic Work*
edited by Leah Scragg

Ben Jonson *Epigrams and The Forest*
edited by Richard Dutton

Giacomo Leopardi *The Canti*
with a selection of his prose
translated by J.G. Nichols

Stéphane Mallarmé *For Anatole's Tomb*
in French and English
translated by Patrick McGuinness

Andrew Marvell *Selected Poems*
edited by Bill Hutchings

Charlotte Mew *Collected Poems and Selected Prose*
edited by Val Warner

Michelangelo *Sonnets*
translated by Elizabeth Jennings,
introduction by Michael Ayrton

William Morris *Selected Poems*
edited by Peter Faulkner

John Henry Newman *Selected Writings to 1845*
edited by Albert Radcliffe

Ovid *Amores*
translated by Tom Bishop

Fernando Pessoa *A Centenary Pessoa*
edited by Eugenio Lisboa and L.C.
Taylor, introduction by Octavio Paz

Petrarch *Canzoniere*
translated by J.G. Nichols

Edgar Allan Poe *Poems and Essays on Poetry*
edited by C.H. Sisson

Restoration Bawdy
edited by John Adlard

Rainer Maria Rilke *Sonnets to Orpheus and Letters to a Young Poet*
translated by Stephen Cohn

Christina Rossetti *Selected Poems*
edited by C.H. Sisson

Dante Gabriel Rossetti *Selected Poems and Translations*
edited by Clive Wilmer

Sir Walter Scott *Selected Poems*
edited by James Reed

Sir Philip Sidney *Selected Writings*
edited by Richard Dutton

John Skelton *Selected Poems*
edited by Gerald Hammond

Charlotte Smith *Selected Poems*
edited by Judith Willson

Henry Howard, Earl of Surrey *Selected Poems*
edited by Dennis Keene

Algernon Charles Swinburne *Selected Poems*
edited by L.M. Findlay

Arthur Symons *Selected Writings*
edited by Roger Holdsworth

William Tyndale *Selected Writings*
edited by David Daniell

Oscar Wilde *Selected Poems*
edited by Malcolm Hicks

William Wordsworth *The Earliest Poems* edited by Duncan Wu

Sir Thomas Wyatt *Selected Poems*
edited by Hardiman Scott

For more information, including a full list of Fyfield*Books* and a contents list for each title, and details of how to order the books in the UK, visit the Fyfield website at www.fyfieldbooks.co.uk or email info@fyfieldbooks.co.uk. For information about Fyfield*Books* available in the United States and Canada, visit the Routledge website at www.routledge-ny.com.